TEARS IN THE Closet

BEING MADE WHOLE THROUGH THE BREAKING PROCESS

Denise Riaño

ISBN 978-1-64492-354-2 (paperback)
ISBN 978-1-64492-355-9 (digital)

Christian Faith Publishing, Inc.
832 Park Avenue
Meadville, PA 16335
www.christianfaithpublishing.com

Printed in the United States of America

CONTENTS

Choose to learn from the pain not be a victim to it!

INTRODUCTION

Broken Pieces Can Be Made Whole in the Hands of the Maker

PITCH-BLACK, DOOR CLOSED, and the only things that surrounded me were my neatly hung clothes and purposely laid-out shoes. I lay there in my small closet, face down on the floor, covered in a flood of tears, coming to terms with the realization that my life had shipwrecked, and there was absolutely nothing that my human efforts could do to fix it.

My closet became my hiding place—the place I would run to in the days ahead to find God, my refuge; the place I completely bared all and began the process of being transformed from the inside out.

In this three-wall dark closet, I discovered that to become the woman God designed me to be—the woman I had desperately desired to be—I would have to go through the valley of the shadow of death.

This is where my journey of transformation began. Come with me, and I will take you through an unforgettable experience that not only changed my life but, I believe, can encourage you in your own healing journey.

I'm writing this book to take you on a life-changing journey and show you through my own experience how God can use your painful seasons to transform your life.

In our journey, I will not only share my struggles, but I will share the strategies and tools God gave me to come out triumphant.

This journey will focus on what I call the transformation pyramid. Each of these stages is carried out through the process by *prayer* (spending time cultivating an intimate relationship with the Lord—*spiritual warfare*), *studying* the Bible (learning who God is, His promises, His nature, and who the Bible says we are), *meditation* (memorizing scriptures, journaling, quiet time with God), and *fasting* (decreasing the power of our flesh and increasing God's power in us).

Stage One: SURRENDER
Stage Two: INTERNAL DETOX
Stage Three: QUIET WALKS THROUGH THE VALLEY
Stage Four: REMADE FROM BROKEN PIECES
Stage Five: THE KEYS TO OVERCOME, GROW, AND LIVE FREE

PRAYER   BIBLE   MEDITATION   FASTING

God led me to write this book in the midst of the most painful season of my life to manifest what He can do when we surrender all to Him, including our deepest pain.

But first, you must decide and be willing to go through and endure the breaking process.

Stage

1

Surrender

It's important to understand that in order to gain
purpose, you have to be willing to sacrifice your
own flesh desires for God's will for your life.

—Tara Jakes, *Faithing It*

NOWHERE TO GO EXCEPT THROUGH THE BREAKING

The most obvious symptom of a soul in need of God's satisfaction is a sense of inner emptiness. The awareness of a "hollow place" somewhere inside. The constant inability to be satisfied.

—Beth Moore, *Breaking Free* devotional
Lifeway Christian Resources

FOR A LONG time, I had a deep-seated yearning for internal wholeness. I wanted to feel and live free from the internal prison I was in since childhood where traumatic experiences held me captive. Innocence was tainted by abuse, neglect, and the absence of love and security. Experiences led my heart to produce an unhealthy self-defense barrier from anyone I perceived was a threat.

Deep down, however, my soul and spirit thirst to be freed from the self that was constantly driven by her emotions and circumstances—from the self-lacking in joy, peace, and contentment. I wanted to feel secure in my God-given purpose—to be the person I was designed to be. My spirit earnestly craved to be quenched by something that, even after a while, did not leave me feeling empty again.

But that's no life for you. You learned Christ! My assumption is that you have paid careful attention to Him, been well instructed in the truth precisely as we have it in Jesus. Hence, we do not have the excuse of ignorance. Everything—and I do mean everything—connected with that old way of life has to go. It's rotten through and through. Get rid of it! And then take on an entirely new way of life—a God-fashioned life—a life renewed from the inside and working itself into your conduct as God accurately reproduces His character in you. (Ephesians 4:20–24, MSG)

I finally got to the point in my life of being sick and tired of being sick and tired. Somehow, I had to embark on the journey of transformation. Then, I came across a Bible devotional called *Streams in the Dessert* (by L.B. Cowman, edited for modern readers by Jim Reimann).

This devotional was one of the most powerful source of strength God had led me to read, for He was well aware of the traitorous process that I would have to endure in the next season of my life. I was going to need the power of His Word to get me through.

One of the expressions that touched my heart profoundly in this devotional was,

> Few Christians are willing to endure the suffering through which complete gentleness is obtained. We must die to ourselves before we are turned into gentleness, and our *Crucifixion* involves suffering. It will mean experiencing genuine brokenness and a crushing of self which will be used to afflict the heart and conquer the mind. (by G.D.W)

Wow! I had to stop and digest every single word. I had to pause at every sentence to allow my heart to grasp the crucial meaning of what G.D.W was describing. I had to come to terms with what it was going to take to go through this painful change in our lives, endure the breaking of everything that ever held me back, and brave the process of loss.

I had to make the decision of yielding my life in submission to the will of God, and be willing to go through the sacrificial exchange, in order to obtain what my true being desperately desired. This meant that my soul had to undergo the affliction of being remade, endure profound anguish, and face my inner most fears, all before I could obtain true wholeness.

So the question I asked myself was, am I willing? Was I willing to surrender all to God without holding anything back? Yes, but it would come at an unimaginable cost—one that would change my life and my family forever.

> Then Jesus said to his disciples, "If any of you wants to be my follower, you must give up your own way, take up your cross, and follow me. If you try to hang on to your life, you will lose it. But if you give up your life for my sake, you will save it. And what do you benefit if you gain the whole world but lose your own soul? Is anything worth more than your soul? (Matthew 16:24–26, NLT)

If you, my friend, have found yourself in the very eye of a traumatic storm, instead of trying desperately to figure a human way out of it, I urge you to STOP. It has a purpose, and the best way to discover what it is, is to go through the breaking process. In the following chapters, I will not only share my own personal experience through this beautifully excruciating transformation, but I will also share principles that can help others navigate through their own difficulties, and be empowered to experience wellness in body, soul, and spirit.

> God can satisfy your yearning soul. Satisfying your innermost places with Jesus is a benefit of the glorious covenant relationship you have with God in Christ. (Beth Moore, *Breaking Free* devotional: Lifeway Christian Resources)

RELINQUISH CONTROL

BEFORE MY VERY eyes, the world I had known for seventeen years was crumbling to bare pieces, and the more it crumbled, the more I held on tight. I thought I could handle it; I thought I knew what I was doing, but the truth was, I was acting foolishly and out of fear. And nothing good ever comes out of acting in fear. The enemy was hiding behind the scenes, studying my every move. He was well aware God had a purpose for me and for my family. And having discovered what I feared most, he went to work in creating a strategy to bring it to pass, and for a period of time, I fell into the trap.

In the attempt to fix my marital problems with my own strength—using my own understanding to figure out the best course of action—things went from bad to worse. It was like trying to extinguish a full-blown fire with oil; even though it's liquid, it's the wrong kind of liquid.

I can tell you, my friend, during this onset part of my process, I was being driven by a swirl of massive emotions that were led by a spirit of fear. I had allowed myself to be engulfed with these emotions so much, I opened the door for the enemy to blind me to his ultimate goal for my family—*division*.

Yes, dividing families is at the forefront of Satan's list, devastating and tearing apart even the people of God. So, my friend, if you find yourself in constant strife with your spouse, children, family members, church members, friends, coworkers, or neighbors, open your eyes and recognize the enemy's tactics to bring division into your life. Because if he can isolate you, he has a better chance at destroying your destiny.

I remember, time and time again, running to my prayer closet begging God to help me, to fix my mess, to make right what had gone wrong. Sometimes, my agony was so fierce, I would shout in loud anguish, hoping for even the smallest amount of relief. In my desperation, I would tell God, He had all the control over my circumstance, but the truth was that every time I left the closet, I would take it right back.

I came face to face with the realization that my will was more important to me than God's will. And because I had decided to allow my emotions to guide me, one of the things I held most dear in my life was torn from me in a blink of an eye. I had foolishly ignored God's warnings; I ignorantly followed my own way and did not heed the guidance and the help of the Holy Spirit.

It was there, at the lowest point of my life—in my closet, face to the floor, tears covering my face, snot coming full-blown out of my nose, and shaken in my emotions—I surrendered. I finally came to the end of the road. I couldn't go back, and the only way to go through was through the valley, relinquishing my hold and giving God full control. Coming to the end of the road, right there and then, I decided to stop playing the "give and take back from God" game. No matter the cost, I was not going back. God knows better than you and I and is the only One who knows how to get us through our darkest hours.

In order for God to come to your rescue, to extend His righteous right hand and lift you out of your pit, you must first stop trying to resolve your own dilemmas. *Relinquish your control and turn it over to Him.*

> In surprising ways, suffering makes room in our spirit for us to know and experience the blessings of God's peace and presence. Without suffering, we simply can't know His comfort. In mourn-

ing, we experience the blessing of God's presence. (Kyle Idleman, *The End of Me: Where Real Life in the Upside-Down Ways of Jesus Begins*, pp. 49–50)

When I began to journey through this terrain of torturous encounters, where every step I took felt as though everything inside of me was coming undone, I was unaware of the hidden treasures, and the undiscovered beauty, that lay within the obscurity of genuine brokenness in the hands of God.

God in His infinite mercy, lavishing His unfailing love on us, takes our shattered pieces—our covered-up brokenness and the messes we make in our lives—and uses it to bring to surface the man/woman we were first designed. God began to use His Word and a series of books and devotionals that empowered me to understand the painful process I was going through. He brought me back to the One who understood better than anyone what it felt to be broken.

He was hated and rejected by people. He had much pain and suffering. People would not even look at him. He was hated, and we didn't even notice him. But he took our suffering on him and felt our pain for us. We saw his suffering and thought God was punishing him (Isaiah 53:3–4, NCV).

Jesus understands the process perfectly. He knows, firsthand, what it means to feel rejected and be torn apart. He sacrificed His own flesh in order to make us whole. There was no way around it for Him; the cross was the only way.

> Sin Judas no hay traición, sin traición no hay arresto, sin arresto no hay azotes, sin azotes no hay cruz, sin cruz no hay muerte, sin muerte no hay resurrección, y sin resurrección no hay victoria. (Yesenia Then, *Mujer Reposicionate*, p. 1187)

Translation:
> Without Judas there is no treason, without treason there is no arrest, without arrest there is no whipping, without whipping there is no

cross, without the cross there is no death, without death there is no resurrection, without resurrection there is no victory. (Yesenia Then, *Mujer Reposicionate,* p. 1187*)*

My friend, if you find yourself in your darkest season today—perhaps the passing of someone dear, maybe a betrayal of trust, the immense struggles of single parenting, the lack in finances, disconnection in a relationship, the trauma of someone taking what was not given, full-blown depression or… I want you to know, you are not alone. You can get through this season and be restored. But before we can become, we must place our wants, desires, and will through the fire to be tested, refined, transformed, and made new, in alignment with Jesus Christ. It is through the sacrifice of our flesh that our true identity is brought to life.

Right here, right now, tell God you are relinquishing all of your control over everything that is hurting you, trusting that as you hand it over to Him, He will have full access to work in your life.

YOU ARE NOT ALONE

THUS FAR, my friends, I have shared with you that if you find yourself in the middle of a difficult situation, the first thing you need to do is stop trying to maneuver your own way out. Instead, *surrender* yourself to God. Once you have gone through that painful step, *relinquish* your control. Give it to the One who can turn your mess into a story—one that will bring hope to all who hear it.

Are these steps easy? *Absolutely not.* This process, this season, this journey, this storm will sometimes feel like you are being torn apart and your pieces are scattered in all directions. There will be times you will feel like you're in a horror film and you can't seem to find your way out. It will test everything you have ever believed and trusted in. BUT, my friend, you are not alone. You have the most magnificent and mighty team on your side; Team Trinity—God the Father, God the Son, and God the Holy Spirit. With them by your side, no matter what comes against you, it will not prosper.

> But the Lord watches over those who fear him, those who rely on his unfailing love. (Psalms 33:18, NLT)

If you stand strong and hold your ground regardless of what you are experiencing in this process—if you don't give up—I guarantee that you will experience God in the most intimate of ways. You will be transformed into a new person, your life will be made new, you will obtain victory, and be blessed like never before.

I will share that as I look back through the sleepless nights and the long agonizing days, I can recall vividly how the pain I was experiencing, felt like sharp glass traveling through my body at high pressure. I'd felt it in my bones, so much so, it would manifest itself in my dreams. I would have clear images of what I was surpassing. I would be crying so bitterly in my dreams, real tears would fall down my eyes. When I woke up the next morning, my face would be wet from all the crying I had done in my dreams.

During the day, I felt like a walking zombie. Everything I did was emotionless, food was tasteless, laughter was nonexistent. I was on autopilot.

But something powerful happens when you have God at the center of your life, and you find yourself falling beneath your load. He shows up every time. And when He comes, you find yourself overcoming difficult obstacles.

Every time I wanted to wrap myself in self-pity or depression, I would think of my daughters and how they needed me to be strong.

Every time I wanted to wallow in hopelessness and give in to the outside pressures, the Holy Spirit reminded me of who I was and who I belonged to.

It was the power and help of the Holy Spirit that did not allow me to drown in despair. In fact, it was by His strength I was able to get up out of bed each morning. The Holy Spirit was the one who nursed me back to health. He didn't give up on me, He nourished me from within, and helped me get through it one step a time, one day at a time.

One of those long nights before I went to sleep, I poured out my aching heart before God. I told Him that I didn't know what to do about my broken marriage and the pain in our daughter's eyes.

"Father, I need your help in making the right decision and respond in a manner that pleases you. In this dark road where there are so many uncertainties, so many things that just don't make sense to the human mind, I desperately need your guidance in how to push forward even if I

can't see the way. Please, Heavenly Father, show me what to do and how to do it. Let me see as you see and do as you say while I'm undergoing this season."

After I finished my prayer, I went to sleep. The next morning when I awoke, I went straight to my prayer closet, closed the door, and in that pitch-black room, I reopened my heart and asked my Father for help.

"I don't want to feel weighed down, imprisoned, and confused about everything, not knowing what to say or how to respond to the test before me and still be transparent no matter what others think. Father, I want to feel love, freedom, peace, and joy no matter what I have to face. I want those four things to be the shield that protect my heart from whatever the enemy throws my way.

Teach me, oh Lord, to be more like Christ. He knew how to act around those who were offensive and around those who rejected him, those who didn't have the same beliefs, those who didn't love him, those who thought differently and lived differently.

I don't want to be known as a religious person. I want to be known for being an encourager, someone who makes a difference with love and compassion. I want to experience true laughter, the kind that doesn't need a mask but expresses itself freely without restrictions, the kind that's free regardless of the circumstances or what others may think. Teach me, Holy Spirit, to be, to act, to respond in freedom. This is my open heart prayer to you my Father, In Jesus name, Amen."

Then I left to go have some breakfast. After I was done, and I came back upstairs, the Holy Spirit lead me to read:

> So, as God's own chosen people, who are holy [set apart, sanctified for His purpose] and well-beloved [by God Himself], put on a heart of compassion, kindness, humility, gentleness, and patience [which has the power to endure whatever injustice or unpleasantness comes, with good temper]. (Colossians 3:12, (AMP))

I mean when I read this, my mouth dropped. And I had to rush, get a pen, and write down what I heard God say to me:

"Denise, I chose you as my own and set you apart for a specific purpose. This is the reason why you have always felt different. This is why you didn't always fit in, like you didn't belong. The enemy has always known how special you are to me, and from the time you were born, he has tried to steal, kill, and destroy your life.

But as my chosen, I have put up a standard around you and your family which he cannot penetrate. He will always come against you and try to overcome you, but he won't succeed. I will always be with you, and my angels will encamp around you to protect you in your coming and your going.

I have heard your cry, I have seen your tears, and I have heard your plea. I am here. You are not alone. I am walking right beside you. As you walk through this process, I want you to treat others with compassion, kindness, humility, gentleness, patience, and forgiveness regardless of what they do or don't do. Always do good and do everything in your power to keep the peace.

These fruits will help you and give you the strength and power to get through whatever difficulty comes your way. They will be a shield against the fiery darts of the devil, and they will protect your heart from those who hurt you. They will help you have the right attitude and response when those closest to you abandon you during your darkest hour. Be at ease, for I am with you.

I won't leave you. Just keep standing no matter what you see and feel.

The Holy Spirit will teach and provide the help you need to put these things into action.

Rest in Me, for I am for you."

You are not alone.

I believe these words were not meant only for me, but for you as well. I believe God knew at this very moment you would be reading this book, and He wanted you to know, He has seen your tears and has heard your prayers. He wants you to take to heart and mind these words: *He is for you, He loves you, and He has a plan for you. You are*

not alone. He is fighting for you and will never abandon you. Put your
trust in Him and let Him bring you out with songs of deliverance.

> You keep track of all my sorrows. You have
> collected all my tears in your bottle. You have
> recorded each one in your book. My enemies will
> retreat when I call to you for help. This I know:
> God is on my side! (Psalms 56:8–9, NLT)

Stage
2
Internal Detox

There is a joy and peace that come only when we finally let ourselves see the pain and let our eyes shed tears for it. Because in the midst of all those tears, all that grief, is where God's blessing can be found.

—Kyle Idleman

PAIN CAN BRING CHANGE

WHEN WE ENCOUNTER some form of trouble in our lives which causes us great pain, the first thing most of us are inclined to do is pray for God to remove it. And although God desires to do that for us, He knows *pain* can bring change.

In a message by Charles Stanley ("God knows the WHY?"), he taught that when storms come in our lives, the source of them are things that either we create ourselves or storms God initiates in our lives or Satan initiates. But regardless of the source of our storm, our response depends on what we believe. One of the promises and fundamental truths we know is that if we are God's children and we love and obey Him, the Bible says that,

> And we know that God causes everything to work together for the good of those who love God and are called according to his purpose for them. (Romans 8:28, NLT)

So no matter where the affliction is coming from, God can use it to remove from our lives things that are a hindrance in our walk with Him and produce in us a character that He can use. God will cause this season of difficulty to work together for your good.

Plainly, in Charles Stanley's words, "Pain purifies our lives."

As I underwent this process of brokenness, I began to seek God so earnestly and intimately in a mission to examine the root causes of the awful pain I had been feeling for so long. And this scripture became an anchor in my prayers:

> Search me, O God, and know my heart; test me and know my anxious thoughts. Point out anything in me that offends you, and lead me along the path of everlasting life. (Psalm 139:23–24, NLT)

I asked God over and over, *"What would you have me do? Look within me Lord and tell what I need to change? Show me the condition of my heart. How can I embrace this awful pain? What is this pain indicating?"*

My friend, I confess that these intimate conversations with the Father were eye-opening experiences that led me to a period of mourning. The Holy Spirit began to reveal rooted behaviors, emotions, and attitudes that I had adopted as my own from childhood experiences, upbringing, and the lack of knowledge of who I truly was. For each of those rooted sins I began to confess, I felt the sharp pains as I came face to face with what each of them had caused in my life and in the lives of others. This journey through confession is critical to the renewal and restoration of our soul and spirit, but we must first make a leap of faith and *embrace the pain.*

On a side note: once you have walked through this valley and grieved, it's important to move forward. We must not wallow in sorrow as if we had no hope in Jesus Christ. We will discuss mourning further in a later chapter.

Isaiah 53 is a chapter in the Old Testament that paints a picture of the gruesome pain Jesus our Savior underwent for the salvation of our lives.

> My servant grew up in the Lord's presence like a tender green shoot, like a root in dry ground. There was nothing beautiful or majestic about

his appearance, nothing to attract us to him. He was despised and rejected—a man of sorrows, acquainted with deepest grief. We turned our backs on him and looked the other way. He was despised, and we did not care. Yet it was our weaknesses he carried; it was our sorrows that weighed him down. And we thought his troubles were a punishment from God, a punishment for his own sins! But he was pierced for our rebellion, crushed for our sins. He was beaten so we could be whole. He was whipped so we could be healed. All of us, like sheep, have strayed away. We have left God's paths to follow our own. Yet the Lord laid on him the sins of us all. He was oppressed and treated harshly, yet he never said a word. He was led like a lamb to the slaughter. And as a sheep is silent before the shearers, he did not open his mouth. Unjustly condemned, he was led away. No one cared that he died without descendants, that his life was cut short in midstream. But he was struck down for the rebellion of my people. He had done no wrong and had never deceived anyone. But he was buried like a criminal; he was put in a rich man's grave. But it was the Lord's good plan to crush him and cause him grief. Yet when his life is made an offering for sin, he will have many descendants. He will enjoy a long life, and the Lord's good plan will prosper in his hands. When he sees all that is accomplished by his anguish, he will be satisfied. And because of his experience, my righteous servant will make it possible for many to be counted righteous, for he will bear all their sins. I will give him the honors of a victorious soldier, because he exposed himself to death. He was counted

among the rebels. He bore the sins of many and
interceded for rebels. (Isaiah 53:2–12, NLT)

No one on earth understands pain like Jesus. Yet, verse 10 says
that "It was the Lord's good plan to crush him and cause him grief."
Right away this tells me that God's good plan for our lives may
involve pain. But if we remain faithful in our trial, we will reap the
rewards that are birthed from our sorrow. "When he sees all that is
accomplished by his anguish, he will be satisfied." This expresses that
if we submit to the will of God, no matter the storms we encounter
in life, God's good plan will bring out blessings that will recreate your
inner world.

> For God called you to do good, even if it means
> suffering, just as Christ suffered for you. He is
> your example, and you must follow in his steps.
> He never sinned, nor ever deceived anyone.
> He did not retaliate when he was insulted, nor
> threaten revenge when he suffered. He left his
> case in the hands of God, who always judges
> fairly. He personally carried our sins in his body
> on the cross so that we can be dead to sin and live
> for what is right. By his wounds you are healed.
> Once you were like sheep who wandered away.
> But now you have turned to your Shepherd, the
> Guardian of your souls. (1 Peter 2:21–25, NLT)

There's no question that in this world you will suffer. Yes, suffer
you will. But WAIT. Don't be alarmed. God has a good plan, and in
Christ, your pain has a beautiful, glorious, and lasting purpose.
Regardless of how many things may seem painful right now,
always remember that you have the "Shepherd, the *guardian* of your
soul" on your side, and His plans are always for you, not against.
I will share that what helped me immensely to self-explore,
learn more about myself, get closer to God, and see the blind spots
in my life was keeping a writing journal which, in turn, birthed this

book. Every time you come before the Father, while you read His Word, read a spirit-nourishing book, or you are spending time alone, have it with you.

If we follow Jesus's example, your pain will be an agent for the kingdom of God. Through the power of the Holy Spirit, God, will begin to deposit insights, desires, greater knowledge, discernment, and enlightened understanding that will awaken you to the purpose of your season.

It's human nature to give into our fight-or-flight internal system and react to our pain by running away from it, suppressing it, placing an invisible bandage on it, or numb the pain with ineffective substances or social distraction. However, if you're willing to really dive in, and examine the source of your pain, then you give God the open door to reveal what you otherwise may not have discovered. Perhaps it's about something you have been putting off, or an incident you've locked away deep in your heart or a habit that's corrupting your life and those around you. Maybe it's about character growth. It may not even be about you, but someone else.

Whatever it may be...God wants to manifest healing, restoration, deliverance, freedom, and make something absolutely new and beautiful in your life.

> My suffering was good for me, for it taught me
> to pay attention to your decrees. (Psalms 119:71
> NLT)

Embracing pain can push us to surrender, drop to our knees, shed tears for the wrong we've done, humble ourselves before God and others, and become vulnerable enough to seek answers and make changes.

Pain drains us of our pride and selfishness and reveals what's really at the core of our hearts.

> So is anyone out there mourning? Where is the
> man who weeps over his selfishness and pride?
> The husband who weeps over his passivity and

the years, lone gone, when he could have led his family? Where is the wife who weeps over her insubmissive and critical spirit? Where is the student who weeps over his cheating, his lust, his ingrained cynicism? Where is the Christian who reads the news and sees the sin in our culture and feels the bruising in his inner spirit? There is a joy and peace that come only when we finally let ourselves see the sin and let our eyes shed tears for it. Because in the midst of all those tears, all that grief, is where God's blessing can be found. (Kyle Idleman, *The End of Me: Where Real Life in the Upside-Down Ways of Jesus Begins*, pp. 59–60)

By choosing to learn from my pain rather than being a victim to it, God was able to show me the things I needed to do in order to let go of old habits and walk in obedience. Embracing pain is not about allowing it to rule your emotions, wrapping yourself in depression and distancing yourself from everything or everyone. It's about allowing yourself to purposefully feel it, in order to discover the answers from within. By finding the hidden treasures of your pain, you'll discover a comfort and a peace that can never be fully grasped with human understanding. In your expedition, if you allow yourself to become vulnerable before God, you'll uncover the all embracing connection with the only One that can give you what your heart has always searched for; Agape love. And trust me when I say, you will experience it in the most beautifully profound ways you have never known.

Pain can be a bridge for you to know God and find your true identity and calling.

In our hands, pain can turn into a big ball of thorns, yet when we give it to God and allow Him to correct, teach, change or remove whatever is making us sick in spirit, He can turn our pain into a beautiful work of art—original and unlike no other.

"Why am I inflicted with this pain?" You may ask! You and I are called to be in the ring, in places where things seem impossible, where we hope against hope having our eyes set on our Author. The life of God in you does not make this life about you but makes you about life to someone around you. Own, integrate, and share your stories bravely cause the world in despair needs you and your story of hope. (Bible devotional (*The Thing About Pain*) by The Light House-Mumbai)

When we have some type of pain in our bodies or when we are physically sick, for the most part, our first inclination is to go visit our primary physician to find out what is wrong and get medication.

Well, similarly, when our heart hurts, we can go to the doctor who created it, find out what is wrong, and what we need to do to become emotionally healthier. The Word of God is the medicine manual. There, He has every type of medication to help you through the pain while He works underneath the heart and in the places you cannot.

You're blessed when you get your inside world—your mind and heart—put right. Then you can see God in the outside world. (Matthew 5:8, MSG)

So while God is working through the details of your life, take hold of the fact that He loves you, and your pain has purpose. If you hold tight to His hands, you'll discover the unseen secrets.

AWAKEN BY CONFESSION AND REPENTANCE

Confession

Oh, what joy for those whose disobedience is forgiven, whose sin is put out of sight! Yes, what joy for those whose record the Lord has cleared of guilt, whose lives are lived in complete honesty! When I refused to confess my sin, my body wasted away, and I groaned all day long. Day and night your hand of discipline was heavy on me. My strength evaporated like water in the summer heat. Finally, I confessed all my sins to you and stopped trying to hide my guilt. I said to myself, "I will confess my rebellion to the Lord." And you forgave me! All my guilt is gone. (Psalm 32:1–5, NLT)

DURING THE BEGINNING stages in my walk through the dark valley, I spent much of my spare time in my prayer closet. It was the place I sought God for comfort, strength, and the answers that only He could provide—the private chamber, I could bare the nakedness of my heart unashamed.

After a time of tug of war with the Lord over what I thought I wanted and needed, I finally came to terms that His way is the only and perfect way. I finally conceded my willingness to follow the road less traveled. It was then when the Holy Spirit led me to the next crucial step in the journey of being transformed—to be spiritually awakened through the process of internal cleansing. Let me explain further:

This part of the valley had to do with stripping away, piece by piece, all the toxic rooted beliefs that had filtered deep within me— the ones that made for themselves permanent residence in my heart with the purpose of rendering me useless.

> Without seeing the depths of sin, we'll never understand the heights of God's love and grace. (Kyle Idleman, *The End of Me: Where Real Life in the Upside-Down Ways of Jesus Begins*, pp. 57–58)

And right there and then, in that dark closet but in the light of Jesus, I was brought to confession. One by one, I felt as though I was yanking out intertwined, deep-seated and overgrown weeds.

With each confession, I felt a release on my inner spirit and with each broken hold, I felt more free. Every layer that was cleansed within me, brought me closer to the core of my true identity.

My friend, it is very important for you to understand that this process is not a one-time approach. It is critical for you to keep in mind that our walk with the Lord on earth is a lifetime process. However, when you are being transformed as you follow God through your darkest valley, there is a unique cleansing that manifests itself internally. During the onset of this undertaking, the Holy Spirit begins to wash away the calluses that have impaired you to live life to your fullest potential. It is through this daring journey that the flesh is put to death, and your spirit is empowered to pursuit the path God has planned for you. It's the process I call "*awakened through confession.*"

There is a death that occurs in this process—a very painful death—the death of your flesh. Yet, at the same time, there is a rebirth. In the light of my confession, I found grace, I found mercy, I found unconditional love and, best of all, forgiveness. My spirit came alive, and the hollow space that once existed in my heart, was filled with the sweet all encompassing love of Jesus.

Again, it was a process.

The Holy Spirit opened my eyes to see each attitude, habit, and character that was displeasing to God. I began to write each one of them in my journal and came face to face with each of them. Through this pathway, I discovered when and how they had latched onto my life and the damage they had caused.

The Holy Spirit helped me to see all the years that they had tormented and deceived me into believing things that were not true. They clouded my mind and made me stumble in my own ignorance. Many times, they kept me isolated, empty, blaming others, and just plain unhappy.

How about you? What poison have you allowed to make its way into your heart and drive your emotions? Lethal words that became rooted as truths—"you are not smart enough," "you will never amount to much," "you will not succeed" "you are damaged goods," "you are not attractive enough," "you are a failure," or that "you don't deserve to be loved or happy." Well, let me stop right here and tell you right now, those beliefs are all BIG FAT LIES. These lies have been making you sick, and this sickness is affecting your relationships and your overall life. And it's time to flush out all that venom out of your system through confession and repentance.

It was through this very painful stage that the tears I shed were able to cleanse the dirt in my eyes. I became vulnerable enough to allow God to expose the dirt that laid hidden deep inside. It was the turning point of finally letting go of my old self and becoming the woman God made me to be.

> There is a certain degree of satisfaction in having the courage to admit one's errors. It not only clears the air of guilt and defensiveness, but often helps solve the problem created by the error. (Dale Carnegie, *How to Win Friends and Influence People*, p. 130)

Therefore, let all the godly pray to you while there is still time, that they may not drown in the floodwaters of judgment. For you are my hiding place; you protect me from trouble. You surround me with songs of victory. (Psalms 32:6–7, NLT)

Repentance

Once we have brought out and laid at the feet of Jesus those things we have allowed to pollute us internally, we must take the next step and *truly repent*. This is a very important step that many of us skim through and, therefore, fail to obtain lasting change.

My friend, without real repentance, your heart and mind will not be able to be transformed into the likeness of Jesus.

If you are not internally remorseful to the point of seeking change in behavior, and the only reason for your confession is simply because you feel sorry for your current state, or to manipulate God into doing something you want, then this step will be in vain.

So repent (change your mind and purpose); turn around and return [to God], that your sins may be erased (blotted out, wiped clean), that times of refreshing (of recovering from the effects of heat, of reviving with fresh air) may come from the presence of the Lord. (Acts 3:19, AMPC)

The active repentance the Word of God calls us to engage in, is bigger than an emotion, it requires action, and it requires change in the way we think and act.

Genuine repentance drives us to purposely acknowledge our wrong thinking, and how it negatively affects every decision we make in our lives.

One of the consequences of sin is that it makes the sinner pity himself instead of causing him to turn to God. One of the first signs of new life is that the individual takes sides with God against himself. (Barnhouse, through Bible commentary "Enduring Word")

I said to myself, "I will watch what I do and not sin in what I say. I will hold my tongue when the ungodly are around me." (Psalm 39:1, NLT)

I placed this verse in my bathroom mirror as a reminder that my words and actions should be an extention of who I am on the inside; a visual call to attention that a clean heart is a healthy heart, one the Lord can intimately commune with.

What does this mean? True repentance leads us to be internally transformed in such a way that it causes us to seek God's will above what we want, what we desire, and what we need. This authentic change will be evident in the way you and I respond to life's challenges.

It means, no matter how painful it is to our flesh, God's will takes precedence each and every time.

Have mercy on me, O God, because of your unfailing love. Because of your great compassion, blot out the stain of my sins. Wash me clean from my guilt. Purify me from my sin. Purify me from my sins, and I will be clean; wash me, and I will be whiter than snow. Create in me a clean heart, O God. Renew a loyal spirit within me. Restore to me the joy of your salvation, and make me willing to obey you. (Psalm 51:1–NLT)

THE PASSAGE THROUGH THE BREAKING IS FORGIVENESS

> Unforgiveness is a strategic "design," craftily implemented by your enemy to "outwit" you, to cripple your effectiveness in prayer and your power to stand against him victoriously. Which is why, if I were your enemy, I would do everything possible to keep you from forgiving anyone and everyone who's done you any wrong. (Priscilla Shirer, *Fervent: A Woman's Battle Plan to Serious, Specific, and Strategic Prayer*)

FOR ME, FORGIVENESS has been an acquired art. It is something that can't be done in haste but, rather, in small strokes. It's definitely a process.

When someone hurts you to the core—to the point your inner spirit moans in agony—forgiveness can seem simply impossible.

That's when unforgiveness comes and knocks at your heart's door disguising itself as the protector. And when it's allowed to enter, it makes itself at home and covers your soul with layers upon layers of lies. The longer it's allowed to stay, the more control it has over our inner self.

As unforgiveness makes itself comfortable in your core, it unloads the most deadly toxins in your body—fear, anxiety, worry, resentment, anger, bitterness, even revenge. It continues until your heart becomes hard and tormented by the stench of betrayal, broken promises, rejection, and feelings of abandonment.

When those who are closest to you turn their backs on you or speak words that feel like a knife slowly ripping through your heart, forgiveness is the last thing you want to think about.

Unforgiveness is a deceiver. And it wants retribution; it wants revenge. It makes us believe that, somehow, partnering up with it is aiding our cause. All the while, it's actually preventing us from receiving the nutrients our spirit needs to thrive. Its main job is to rob us of God's blessing for our lives.

When unforgiveness gets a hold of your heart, it begins to steer your thoughts, emotions, attitude, and actions in the opposite direction God wants you to go. It will cause you greater pain than the one done to you. It will isolate you, destroy relationships, and ultimately, your overall wellness.

Therefore, the antidote for a broken heart is always forgiveness. It is the only true way to get through your breaking process and come out completely healed, delivered, and set free.

Forgiveness is the key to having real peace in your heart.

It's the medicine to a healthy soul.

So how do we forgive? How do we deal with the pain others have caused? How do we forgive ourselves? Well, for starters, we can't do it on our own; we need the help of the Holy Spirit.

We need to open up, be truthful about what and how we feel, and ask Him to help us forgive, to help us give ourselves grace and room for our imperfections, remembering that Jesus came for that very purpose. He knew we would need someone to intercede on our behalf during those times we sin against God.

We ask the Holy Spirit to help us pray for that person that offended or hurt us, to help us understand and have compassion over them, and to see them as God sees them.

When we genuinely pray in this way, we are aligning our will with God's will and, thus, opening the door for God's favor and blessings in our lives.

But when you are praying, first forgive anyone you are holding a grudge against, so that your Father in heaven will forgive your sins too. (Mark 11:25, NLT)

You may say, "No way, it's too difficult! You have no idea what I've done, or you can't even imagine what they did!" Yes, I can relate in many ways. Forgiving myself has been one of the hardest thing to do, not to mention those who have hurt me deeply. Nevertheless, my friend, worse was done to Jesus, and even while He was on the cross, He said these words:

Jesus said, "Father, forgive them, for they don't know what they are doing." (Luke 23:34, NLT)

We can also change the way we view forgiveness. The Word of God says that we need to.

Guard your heart above all else, for it determines the course of your life." (Proverbs 4:23, NLT)

* When we intentionally keep in mind that what is in our hearts * is guiding our lives and determines how we live, how we respond and, ultimately, our future, we can be proactive in making sure our hearts stay clean.
* We intentionally live out each day making sure the only person that rules over our lives is God, and the only thing that is covering our hearts is love. *

Any fool can criticize, condemn and complain and most fools do. But it takes character and self-control to be understanding and forgiving. (Dale Carnegie)

Be intentional about what is in my heart. Character + self control

37

It is imperative to always be ready to forgive

Let's look at a great example of this in the Bible.

> "Why are you so angry?" the Lord asked Cain.
> "Why do you look so dejected? You will be
> accepted if you do what is right. But if you refuse
> to do what is right, then watch out! Sin is crouch-
> ing at the door, eager to control you. But you
> must subdue it and be its master." (Genesis 4:6–
> 7, NLT)
>
> God warned Cain about the destructive
> power of sin. Cain could have resisted sin and
> found blessing, or he could give in to sin and be
> devoured. We prevent sin from ruling over us by
> allowing God to master us first. Without God as
> our master, we will be slaves to sin. (Enduring
> Word)

Sin never rests. It is always looking for an opportunity to control us, to deceive us, and make us fall.*That is why it is <u>imperative</u>
that we are always ready to forgive no matter what, because when we
do, we are taking authority over it and mastering it. *

We have to shift the perspective on forgiveness and remember
that it has been freely given from God. That it's not only a command
but also an emulation of what He did for us through His son Jesus
Christ for the forgiveness of our own sins.

But even more, the Bible says that,

> If you forgive those who sin against you, your
> heavenly Father will forgive you. But if you refuse
> to forgive others, your Father will not forgive
> your sins. (Matthew 6:14–5, NLT)

So, my friend, don't allow anything or anyone to come between
you and God. Period. Changing the way we see forgiveness will
enable us to guard our hearts, our ability to hear from God, our overall health, and the direction of our lives.

When we forgive, we aren't dismissing the pain or betrayal that's taken place. We release the offense to a God who is no stranger to pain or betrayal. Forgiveness declares that grace is greater than bitterness or resentment. It doesn't give a shred of power to our offender. It sets us free. (Tiffany Bluhm, *Flourish: 21 Ways to Thrive Before 45*)

These are just some of the scriptures that talk about FORGIVENESS:

Make allowance for each other's faults and forgive anyone who offends you. Remember, the Lord forgave you, so you must forgive others. (Colossians 3:13, NLT)

So watch yourselves! If another believer sins, rebuke that person; then if there is repentance, forgive. Even if that person wrongs you seven times a day and each time turns again and asks forgiveness, you must forgive. (Luke 17:3–4, NLT)

Get rid of all bitterness, rage, anger, harsh words, and slander, as well as all types of evil behavior. Instead, be kind to each other, tenderhearted, forgiving one another, just as God through Christ has forgiven you. (Ephesians 4:31–32, NLT)

I—yes, I alone—will blot out your sins for my own sake and will never think of them again. Let us review the situation together, and you can present your case to prove your innocence. (Isaiah 43:25–26, NLT)

Now repent of your sins and turn to God, so that your sins may be wiped away. (Acts 3:19, NLT)

He has removed our sins as far from us as the east is from the west. (Psalms 103:12, NLT)

But if we confess our sins to him, he is faithful and just to forgive us our sins and to cleanse us from all wickedness. (1 John 1:9, NLT)

Stage

3

Quiet Walks through the Valley

Everything changes when we see weakness and suffering in the light of the gospel. For it is through human weakness that God's strength upholds us and is displayed to the world.
—Kristen Wetherell and Sarah Walton

$\mathcal{G}$UARD YOUR MIND

DR. CAROLINE LEAF, a Christian Cognitive Neuroscientist, says that, "If you learn to think, you will find God."

She discusses in her book, *Switch On Your Brain: The Key to Peak Happiness, Thinking, and Health*," how the body nor the brain have the ability to choose. Our mind and our spirit can express themselves through our brain and our bodies. Every word that you say and every action you perform is, first, a thought in your head.

After studying this book, I began to pay close attention to my thought process and how it affected me as a whole. I quickly noticed that when I allowed my mind to roam free, toxic thoughts would manifest in initiating feelings of anxiousness, worry, fear, confusion, anger, etc. These emotions in turn, affected my attitude and my behavior negatively.

Dr. Leaf goes on to say that,

> As we think, we change the physical nature of our brain. As we consciously direct our thinking, we can wire out toxic patterns of thinking and replace them with healthy thoughts. New thought networks grow. We increase our intelligence and bring healing to our brains, minds, and physical bodies. It all starts in the realm of

the mind, with our ability to think and choose—
the most powerful thing in the universe after
God, and indeed, fashioned after God.

Having gained this knowledge, I intentionally sought the help
of the Holy Spirit to empower me and teach my mind to purposely
run to the Word of God, a Christian book, Biblical teaching, or worship music, to combat the surge of negative thoughts and emotions.
Then, when I saw how implementing this mind-renewal process
brought a sense of peace, tranquility, and hope, I began to do it con-
sistently until it became habit.

My new motto: feel pain—seek God.

It brings instant peace to the mind. The Word of God says,

How shall a young man cleanse his way? By taking heed and keeping watch [on himself] according to Your word [conforming his life to it].
(Psalm 119:9, AMPC)

The questions then becomes: Do you want to remove thoughts
that cause depression, despair, hopelessness, confusion, discouragement, bitterness, self-pity, etc.? Do you want to be able to regulate
your thought process and not allow the enemy access over your
mind? Do you want to have a thought process that functions on the
grace and freedom of Christ? In other words, do you want the mind
of Christ? Then you need to become armed with the Word of God
and go to work. Stand your ground at the entrance of your mind,
diligently "keeping watch" of what comes in and out, making sure
the enemy's lies do not have even a crack to break-in.

Doing this revokes Satan's power to filter through our minds
and plant deceptions that only bring fear and disconnection from
God.

How often must we do this process? DAILY—from the time you
arise to the time you lie down. Never allow the doors of your mind
unguarded. We need to keep watch.

The enemy is ceaselessly looking for an opportunity to infiltrate. To combat his tactics, we need to have the Word of God imprinted in our minds, speak it over ourselves and those we pray for.

Dr. Leaf further explains,

> Good thinking = good choices = healthy thoughts; Toxic thinking = toxic choices = toxic thoughts. You are designed to stand outside yourself and observe your own thinking and change it. You are designed to recognize and choose the right things to think about. Each morning when you wake up, you have new baby nerve cells born inside your brain to use wisely as you remove bad thoughts and wire in new ones.

I believe many people spend a great deal of time thinking about the past and mourning about what they could have done differently. These toxic thoughts of regret bombard the mind with such coercion that if allowed, they end up in our soul, becoming a part of our believe system and confessions.

These negative thoughts, if left unchecked, can produce a ripple effect that will hinder our walk with God, our full potential, obtaining desired goals and, ultimately, our destiny. I became very well aware that the more I sought God and the more I used what I had to serve Him, the more the enemy would come full force and attack my mind. I felt the oppression so intensely, my bones would ache. Sometimes, the attack was so strong, I often struggled to get dressed in the morning, and I could fill buckets of all the tears I cried in secret.

Internally, I felt like I was in a 24/7 boxing match; My flesh and my spirit fighting for full control. I realized that the one I fed the most, was the champion that day.

> Keep a cool head. Stay alert. The Devil is poised to pounce, and would like nothing better than to catch you napping. Keep your guard up. You're

not the only ones plunged into these hard times. It's the same with Christians all over the world. So keep a firm grip on the faith. The suffering won't last forever. It won't be long before this generous God who has great plans for us in Christ— eternal and glorious plans they are—will have you put together and on your feet for good. He gets the last word; yes, he does. (1 Peter 5:8–11, MSG)

The enemy wants us neutralized. He does not want us using our abilities to help and encourage others. He does not want us getting in the way of his mission, blinding people to their true identity and purpose. No, he wants you and me down, depressed, in despair, weak, and most of all, SILENT. But, my friends, we must not succumb to his cunning tactics, rather, we need to relentlessly clutch ever more our trust and focus on Jesus. We hold tightly to God's Word, and no matter what Satan throws our way, we won't falter. We stand unmovable, believing the promises of God for rescue and deliverance. For "He gets the last word."

Therefore if you have been raised with Christ [to a new life, sharing in His resurrection from the dead], keep seeking the things that are above, where Christ is, seated at the right hand of God. Set your mind and keep focused habitually on the things above [the heavenly things], not on things that are on the earth [which have only temporal value]. (Colossians 3:1–2, AMP)

How? You ask, do we keep our mind on heavenly things when everything around us seem to be falling apart?

I have discovered that during the times when I felt most anxious and fearful, instead of giving into the emotions they evoked, I took a time-out, went to a quiet place, and I gave into God. That simple act of surrender opens the door for God's healing. Ask the Holy Spirit to replace the hindering thoughts with His powerful presence. His presence has the power to change anything, including our minds. Why? Because God's presence brings forth true love, joy, peace, and everything you need to reposition your soul on things that are eternal.

> And do not be conformed to this world [any longer with its superficial values and customs], but be transformed and progressively changed [as you mature spiritually] by the renewing of your mind [focusing on godly values and ethical attitudes], so that you may prove [for yourselves] what the will of God is, that which is good and acceptable and perfect [in His plan and purpose for you]. (Romans 12:2, AMP)

Renewing your mind is not only a process that takes time, it is also a process that needs to take place throughout our day.

The process of renewal is more effective when done in strides; replacing one negative habit at a time with a positive one. And this takes commitment. A commitment that can be achieved in partnership with the Holy Spirit and bathing yourself in God's Word.

One of the best ways to get rid of toxic thinking is by declaring God's Word over your life out loud, and if you can do it in front of a mirror, even better. Because death and life is in the power of the tongue, we can bring life to our thinking by declaring God's truth over our minds. God's Word, when spoken in faith, in truth, and with authority, responds like a sharp sword covered in flames. The enemy has no choice but to flee the scene of our minds.

> The biggest lesson I have ever learned is the stupendous importance of what we think. If I knew what you think, I would know what you are, for your thoughts make you what you are. By changing our thoughts, we can change our lives. (Dale Carnegie)

PRAISE EVEN IN THE VALLEY

WOKE UP THIS morning feeling weighed down. I felt a swirl of emotions heading in opposite directions. The one that was gripping me the most was loneliness. I felt utterly alone and in desperate need of just being held and told how much I was loved. So I did the only thing I knew to do, I went to the Father.

At first, I found it very difficult to even open my mouth. My emotions were urging me to go back to bed, to put the covers over my head, and cry myself back to sleep, but my spirit resisted. I knew deep inside me what was happening, and I needed to fight.

I remembered the scripture,

> But thou art holy, O thou that inhabitest the praises of Israel. (Psalm 22:3, KJV)

and the words of author Linda W. Rooks (*Broken Heart on Hold*):

> God is with us always—in our everyday life, in our pain, in our joys, in our prayerful suppli-cations. But He inhabits our praise. When we praise Him, it opens up our hearts, and gives

God permission to revive the very depths of our inner-being.

So I pushed myself past the discord in my flesh, and I opened my heart to God with the help of His Word.

I began to praise God with Psalm 145. It was definitely a sacrificial praise.

But something happens internally when we overcome our flesh. It's like holding your breath underwater for a long time and then finally coming up for air; What do you feel? Relief.

That's how I felt. I was relieved of my burden and, in exchange, received God's reassuring peace.

I knew my heart was open because the weight of my circumstances began to lift, the whirlwind of thoughts in my mind began to cease, and my emotions became still; God had come in. His presence calmed the chaos within me and filled my empty space.

> I will praise the Lord at all times. I will constantly speak his praises. (Psalms 34:1, NLT)

Tears began to flow and I was able to commune with the Father with freedom and honesty. He gave me, not what my flesh wanted but what my spirit hungrily needed—His love, His presence, His comfort, His strength, His acceptance and, more importantly, His peace. It's the way He designed us; Only His unmatched provisions can truly quench the cravings of our inner being.

After this beautiful encounter, my Heavenly Father led me to read a devotional in *Streams in the Desert* that said,

> "Left alone!" What different emotions these words bring to mind for each of us! To some they mean loneliness and grief, but to others they may mean rest and quiet. To be left alone without God would be too horrible for words, while being left alone with him is a taste of heaven! And if his

followers spent more time alone with him, we would have spiritual giants again.

Earnestly desire to get alone with God. If we neglect to do so, we not only rob ourselves of a blessing but we rob others as well, since we will have no blessing to pass on to them. It may mean that we do less outward, visible work, but the work we do will have more depth and power. Another wonderful result will be that people will see "no one except Jesus" (Matthew 17:8) in our lives.

The impact of being alone with God in prayer cannot be overemphasized.

No matter what I face in life, I can't ever stop getting alone with God. I can't allow my thoughts or emotions steer me away from Him by giving into pain and fear.

> For it is [not your strength, but it is] God who is effectively at work in you, both to will and to work [that is, strengthening, energizing, and creating in you the longing and the ability to fulfill your purpose] for His good pleasure. (Philippians 2:13, AMP)

I believe we all face moments in life when we feel utterly helpless as though we are backed up in a dark corner, nowhere we can run to for escape and no one to turn to for help.

Where we utter the words, "I just can't do this," and are tempted to question God and turn to other means to deal with our frustrations, all in the hopes to find sanity.

However, if we are not careful, we can fall into the enemy's trap of closing us off from the flow that goes from the Vine (Jesus) to the branch (us). He is a master at making the illusion that our circumstances are worse than they really are.

He wants your heart to became hard and closed. Be AWARE; he will do whatever it takes to deceive you into thinking you are all alone and no one, including God, understands or cares. *He is a big fat liar.*

Because God reminds us time and time again that,

> The Lord is close to all who call on him, yes, to all who call on him in truth. He grants the desires of those who fear him; he hears their cries for help and rescues them. (Psalm 145:18–19 NLT)

So we need to tell Satan to take his lies and take a hike.

Our hearts belong to God, and if we keep praise on our mouths, His presence will always come near to us.

There are so many things my heart desires, but right now, right now, all I need is alone time with the Lord. The best thing I can do for my life, my family, and others is to be still and embrace my Father's warmth and His sweet whispers. For it is in His presence that I am clothed with all that I need to fulfill my purpose in the land of the living.

WAITING WITH HUMBLE PATIENCE AND FAITHFUL EXPECTATION

ONE OF THE most difficult seasons in a person's life is the season of *waiting*.

We live in a society where so much of our everyday life has been catered to us by the push of a button. From drive-throughs, express lines, deliveries, instant meals, online orders through the famous apps Alexa and Google, all for the purpose of instant gratification and the avoidance of the intolerable feeling of *waiting*.

Our flesh does not easily accept situations that are not under its control. Our flesh does whatever it must to avoid feeling uncomfortable. We have a hard time dealing with the unknowns, with the what if's, with the silence that forces us to be with ourselves. When we encounter situations where we feel forced to wait, sometimes attitudes and behaviors that are out of character can emerge. Yes, it's happened to me.

The point is that we all deal with the process of waiting differently, but my reason for this chapter is how to wait in a manner that helps us grow in character and, ultimately, please God.

In a study by Kate Sweeny, an associate professor of psychology at the University of California Riverside, they found that having an optimistic outlook and being more comfortable with uncertainty helped people handle waiting periods better (*Time* magazine article by Alice Park, December 5, 2014, "Here's How to Make Waiting A Little Less Excruciating").

For me, this means that an attitude that displays humbleness, patience, and realistic expectation is able to go through the process of waiting more successfully.

In my own personal walk, the process of waiting through the uncertainties of what would become of my marriage and family was one of the hardest thing I've had to endure; nevertheless, it was the one that brought the most reward. Let me explain.

There were times in my life where I was called to wait, yet I did it with the wrong attitude. Viewing waiting as something was being withheld from me, enticed me to become impatient, have a negative attitude, and respond incorrectly.

Why did I react to waiting with indignation? At the very core, I discovered that it was fear not faith that held my heart. When we become restless over our circumstance, we are simply saying we don't trust God to handle it.

> "The only thing that can be said to restrain God is our unbelief" (Matthew 13:58). God's power is never restrained but His will may be restrained by our unbelief. He may choose not to act until we partner with Him in trust. (David Guzik)

When we lose our trust in God (as I often did) and allow unruly emotions like impatience to lead us, we end up making decisions that can oftentimes result in regret. When we choose to go ahead of God because we don't see things working as fast as we think they should, or we don't see with our carnal eyes the results we want, we make for ourselves an idol just like the people of Israel did when Moses went up to the Mountain of Sinai.

> Then the Lord said to Moses, "Come up to me on the mountain. Stay there, and I will give you the tablets of stone on which I have inscribed the instructions and commands so you can teach

the people." So Moses and his assistant Joshua set out, and Moses climbed up the mountain of God. Moses told the elders, "Stay here and wait for us until we come back. Aaron and Hur are here with you. If anyone has a dispute while I am gone, consult with them." Then Moses climbed up the mountain, and the cloud covered it. And the glory of the Lord settled down on Mount Sinai, and the cloud covered it for six days. On the seventh day the Lord called to Moses from inside the cloud. To the Israelites at the foot of the mountain, the glory of the Lord appeared at the summit like a consuming fire. Then Moses disappeared into the cloud as he climbed higher up the mountain. He remained on the mountain forty days and forty nights. (Exodus 24:12–18, NLT)

There will be times in our lives when God will call us to a time of separation from all to be alone in His presence. The length of time will not be measured by our standards, for God, though loving and compassionate, is not moved by our level of comfort but the growth in our character. There is a very specific and intimate process that occurs only when we are set apart and are alone in His presence.

Just like Moses, the Lord calls each and every one of us to go away with Him for a period of time where, in many instances, a transaction takes place. For me this transaction, involved the complete surrender of my will, my past, my sins, my hurts, my guilt and shame, my unforgiveness, my all. And in response, the Lord gave me Himself; which is everything I could ever need in One.

During this period of time, I literally felt like I was being stripped of all those attitudes that brought nothing but pain and distance from the Lord. And because of my submission, God was able to unveil from within my soul, my true identity and the purpose I was born to pursue and accomplish.

But personal growth takes time. It takes patience and yes, much self-compassion. Did I fumble during this process? Absolutely! especially in the beginning. I lacked trust. This, however, was one of the greatest treasures that can be build in us through this time of waiting. There are certain aspects of our lives that can only be brought forth through the period of waiting.

Let me show you:

> When the people saw how long it was taking Moses to come back down the mountain, they gathered around Aaron. "Come on," they said, "make us some gods who can lead us. We don't know what happened to this fellow Moses, who brought us here from the land of Egypt." The Lord told Moses, "Quick! Go down the mountain! Your people whom you brought from the land of Egypt have corrupted themselves. How quickly they have turned away from the way I commanded them to live! They have melted down gold and made a calf, and they have bowed down and sacrificed to it. They are saying, 'These are your gods, O Israel, who brought you out of the land of Egypt.'" (Exodus 32:1, 7–8, NLT)

The people of Israel became impatient, and decided to forsake all that God had done for them, and what God had instructed them to do. They preferred to go back to their old ways, to trust in what they knew, to do whatever it took to satisfying the flesh and not feel uncomfortable. By doing this, they disobeyed God, they hurt and angered God, and eventually, they brought destruction upon their lives.

I believe God uses the period of waiting to test our faith, our obedience, our commitment, our allegiance, and to reveal the true nature of our hearts. He also uses this period to build our trust in Him, to see how we respond, and what He represents in our lives.

Certain of God's people are in trouble and distress, and they are eager for immediate rescue. They cannot wait God's time, nor exercise submission to his will. He will surely deliver them in due season; but they cannot tarry till the hour cometh; like children, they snatch at unripe fruit. "To everything there is a season, and a time to every purpose under the heaven," but their one season is the present; they cannot, they will not wait. They must have their desire instantaneously fulfilled, or else they are ready to take wrong means of attaining it. If in poverty, they are in haste to be rich; and they shall not long be innocent. If under reproach, their heart ferments toward revenge. They would sooner rush under the guidance of Satan into some questionable policy, than in childlike simplicity trust in the Lord and do good. It must not be so with you, my brethren, you must learn a better way. (Spurgeon)

So then this brings us to the question of how do we WAIT in the way that pleases God?

By waiting with an attitude of humble patience and faithful expectation.

Easy to say, but for some, seemingly impossible. But thanks be to Jesus Christ for sending us the Helper, the Holy Spirit, who holds that very essence (the fruit) within him to enable us to obtain it and do all those things that seem too great for us to conquer.

Now you may say; "yes, yes, I know Denise, you've said this before," yet I can't stress enough how critically important is His indwelling. Even our Lord Jesus said that it was necessary for Him to go to the Father in order that the Holy Spirit may come to help us in every area of our lives.

So I say, let the Holy Spirit guide your lives. Then you won't be doing what your sinful nature craves. The sinful nature wants to do evil, which is just the opposite of what the Spirit wants. And the Spirit gives us desires that are the opposite of what the sinful nature desires. These two forces are constantly fighting each other, so you are not free to carry out your good intentions. But when you are directed by the Spirit, you are not under obligation to the law of Moses. When you follow the desires of your sinful nature, the results are very clear: sexual immorality, impurity, lustful pleasures, idolatry, sorcery, hostility, quarreling, jealousy, outbursts of anger, selfish ambition, dissension, division, envy, drunkenness, wild parties, and other sins like these. Let me tell you again, as I have before, that anyone living that sort of life will not inherit the Kingdom of God. But the Holy Spirit produces this kind of fruit in our lives: love, joy, peace, patience, kindness, goodness, faithfulness, gentleness, and self-control. There is no law against these things! (Galatians 5:16–23, NLT)

As long as we live on this earth, there will always be an internal war where the Spirit of God must win in order for us to fulfill our purpose on this earth.

How? We must yield to the Holy Spirit daily by growing an intimate relationship with Him. He was sent to be our Helper, and He has the power to equip us with whatever we need to live godly and victoriously; But first yield to Him.

The Holy Spirit reminds us that the Lord is our 24/7 head physician on call. And when we are hurting, He immediately draws near. Extracting our pain and mending the broken pieces with His deep affectionate love. Waiting can be wearisome, and we may be tempted to give up. Simply don't. We must trust that waiting patiently will honor God and bring things to pass for His glory and for our good.

There are things that the Lord is doing and shifting in the spiritual realm that we can't see. There are preparations, transformations, and character building that need to take place before we see our already answered prayer. But there is no way around it, we must first *wait patiently.*

Waiting with the right posture can provide us the time we need to work on ourselves and to grow personally and spiritually, allowing God to work things out for a greater purpose. The second principle to acquire the ability to wait with humble patience and faithful expectancy is by fully trusting in God.

Here is another time when impatience and lack of trust in God led to disobedience of man and the withdrawal of a blessing:

> Some of them crossed the Jordan River and escaped into the land of Gad and Gilead. Meanwhile, Saul stayed at Gilgal, and his men were trembling with fear. Saul waited there seven days for Samuel, as Samuel had instructed him earlier, but Samuel still didn't come. Saul realized that his troops were rapidly slipping away. So he demanded, "Bring me the burnt offering and the peace offerings!" And Saul sacrificed the burnt offering himself. Just as Saul was finishing with the burnt offering, Samuel arrived. Saul went out to meet and welcome him, but Samuel said, "What is this you have done?" Saul replied, "I saw my men scattering from me, and you didn't arrive when you said you would, and the Philistines are at Michmash ready for battle. So I said, 'The Philistines are ready to march against us at Gilgal, and I haven't even asked for the Lord's help!' So I felt compelled to offer the burnt offering myself before you came." "How foolish!" Samuel exclaimed. "You have not kept the command the Lord your God gave you. Had you kept it, the Lord would have established

your kingdom over Israel forever. But now your kingdom must end, for the Lord has sought out a man after his own heart. The Lord has already appointed him to be the leader of his people, because you have not kept the Lord's command." (1 Samuel 13:7–14, NLT)

I have, many times, gone ahead of God and made very "stupid" decisions that have consequently brought unavoidable problems. Sometimes, we make idols out of the opinions of other people and make choices based on the fear of what they might think or say about us, when ultimately, the only person we should be most concerned about offending and hurting is God. His timing is always perfect, and when we wait, His blessings are always worth the wait.

You may ask, "How do I trust a God I can't see?"

I will tell you what I did that helped me believe in Him even when everything around me was falling apart, and my path became pitch black.

Ready? By reading and studying the Old Testament.

You say, "What? What does the Old Testament have to do with trust or faith in God?"

In order to trust someone, you must know who they truly are, and the Old Testament gives us a clear picture on the true character and nature of *who* God is by the way He fellowshipped with His people throughout history. We can make connections between what He has done in the past with what He is doing now.

Let me show you another story in the Old Testament where God blessed beyond expectation, and demonstrated love and compassion to a woman's pleas during her time of humble patience and faithful expectation.

So Hannah arose after they had finished eating and drinking in Shiloh. Now Eli the priest was sitting on the seat by the doorpost of the tabernacle of the Lord. And she was in bitterness of soul, and prayed to the Lord and wept in anguish. Then she made a vow and said, "O Lord of hosts, if You will indeed look on the affliction of Your maidservant and remember me, and not forget Your maidservant, but will give Your maidservant a male child, then I will give him to the Lord all the days of his life, and no razor shall come upon his head." And it happened, as she continued praying before the Lord, that Eli watched her mouth. Now Hannah spoke in her heart; only her lips moved, but her voice was not heard. Therefore, Eli thought she was drunk. So Eli said to her, "How long will you be drunk? Put your wine away from you!" But Hannah answered and said, "No, my lord, I am a woman of sorrowful spirit. I have drunk neither wine nor intoxicating drink, but have poured out my soul before the Lord. Do not consider your maidservant a wicked woman, for out of the abundance of my complaint and grief I have spoken until now." Then Eli answered and said, "Go in peace, and the God of Israel grant your petition which you have asked of Him." And she said, "Let your maidservant find favor in your sight." So the woman went her way and ate, and her face was no longer sad. Then they rose early in the morning and worshiped before the Lord, and returned and came to their house at Ramah. And Elkanah knew Hannah his wife, and the Lord remembered her. So it came to pass in the process of time that Hannah conceived and bore a son, and called his name Samuel, saying, "Because I have asked for him from the Lord." (1 Samuel 1:9–20, NKJV)

And Eli would bless Elkanah and his wife, and say, "The Lord give you descendants from this woman for the loan that was given to the

Lord." Then they would go to their own home. And the Lord visited Hannah, so that she conceived and bore three sons and two daughters. Meanwhile the child Samuel grew before the Lord. (1 Samuel 2:20–21, NKJV)

Not only did God grant Hanna a child, but He went beyond her expectations—beyond what she had asked or thought—and gave her five more children.

God honored her humble attitude during her waiting period, and after she had left her request at the altar, while waiting expectantly for His answer.

What does all this mean? Well, God wants us to know that He sees, feels, and understands our deep sadness. It's perfectly normal. He is very attuned to the twists and turns we encounter in life. Nevertheless, He also understands how important it is for our spiritual growth to learn to trust Him no matter how difficult the situation might present itself. He is very well aware of our hearts desire; it is for that very reason, we must learn to wait humbly and expectantly.

Though this journey is nonnegotiable, if we want the blessings God promises to those who obey and trust in Him, we must learn to endure and wait under His protective mantle, as we leave our petitions at the altar. We must learn to allow Him to soothe our soul's yearnings and delight solely in His presence.

I waited patiently for the Lord to help me, and he turned to me and heard my cry. He lifted me out of the pit of despair, out of the mud and the mire. He set my feet on solid ground and steadied me as I walked along. He has given me a new song to sing, a hymn of praise to our God. Many will see what he has done and be amazed. They will put their trust in the Lord. (Psalms 40:1–3, NLT)

Our Heavenly Father has promised to be with each and one of us every step of the way, even more on those days our heart is stricken with solemn distress. We must not allow our circumstances to bridge a gap between God and us, instead, when hopelessness tries to wedge itself into our hearts, we need to run to Him. He is the "lamp to your feet" and the "light to your path." His love and blessing will cover us as we wait with the right attitude for His help.

> God's foundations are steady and when we have
> His patience within, we are steady while we wait.
> (C.H.P., *Streams in the Desert*)

WALKING FORWARD WITH PURPOSE

> Too much introspection into your problems and
> weaknesses can cause you to become ingrown.
> You can turn inward and over time cause great
> damage to yourself, all in the name of trying to
> know yourself or fix your problems. The best cure
> for many emotional difficulties is to turn out-
> ward and start giving to others. (Charles Stanley,
> devotional, *Seven Keys to Emotional Wholeness*)

AS MY SEASON continued to unfold, I found myself doing just
that—turning to seclusion, avoiding being with people, staying home
more often, and spending much of my time closed in my room.

There were so many days when I struggled to leave my house
and go to church or work. With my heart full of gloom, I didn't
feel capable of giving of myself. But through the encouragements
and prayers of caring friends, loving mother, church family and, of
course, my best friend, the Holy Spirit, I always had the strength to
push past my own internal restraints and walk forward with purpose.

I learned that when you are at your worst, the best thing you
can do is help someone else. I did whatever I could or was led by God
to do in the service of others. Whether it was with a smile, an encouragement, monetary, food or clothing donations, or through volun-

teering, I made it my purpose to help someone else. WHY? Because when I helped someone else, I felt inner joy and satisfaction. It's an indescribable feeling when you can push pass the hurdle of your own pain for the sake of helping another person; I believe it's a gift from God.

It wasn't always easy. Many times, I just wanted to hide myself away, but the Holy Spirit always reminded me of my assignment. He would remind me that there are people out there who need my help, and I needed to stop feeling sorry for myself, go forth, and walk with the purpose I had been designed with.

This was a daily prompting. I would leave my house on a mission to bless someone in some way. Walking in my purpose, serving, and using my resources to bless others brought me true fulfillment even in the midst of deep emotional heartbreak and separation in my marriage.

I always tried to keep in mind that my life represented God, and I needed to live out my faith even when the chaos in my life did not make sense. I had to walk with integrity and show my daughters that we serve and obey God no matter the season, the difficulty, or the state of our emotions because, no matter what, we are children of God, and our lives belong to Him.

In the Bible, we learn of a woman who had experienced much tragedy in her life, and though very distraught, she decided to move forward with the purpose of returning back to where she should have never left.

In the book of Ruth, Naomi and her family left their homeland of Bethlehem to go to the country of Moab in search for a better life, but instead, she found pain and misery. After the death of her husband and two sons, she was left a widow and childless.

Naomi could have stayed and indulged herself in misfortune and grief the rest of her life. She could have waited bitterly for the day where she, too, would turn to dust; However, she never forgot who she was nor the God of her people. I believe Naomi strengthened herself in the recollections of all that God had done for her people. She knew she could no longer stay in a state of dissolution. She had to pack up and move forward with the purpose of realigning herself with God's will. Had Naomi not gone back to Bethlehem, Ruth, her daughter-in-law who went with her, would have never met Boaz; and if she had never met Boaz, then Jesse would have never been born, which means, nor David would have been born and so on. In fact, Jesus Christ our Lord and Savior is of this very lineage.

Naomi had been born with a purpose. Even though she had derailed from it for a period of time, God never abandoned her, and He guided her footsteps back into His perfect plan.

No matter what you are going through or how sorrowful or hopeless the situation may seem, don't make your home there. You must girdle yourself with strength by remembering God's goodness, and all that He has done in your life, then use it as an anchor to propel forward in purpose. Utilize what you have; gifts, abilities, talents, time, and resources, in the place you are in right now, and with the help of the Holy Spirit, GO…fulfill God's assignment for your life, even if you are in the middle of a mess. That's called sacrificial praise. In those days when you don't feel like serving or can barely open your mouth to say the expected "I'm good thank you," just give a smile or a hug instead. And that sacrificial act in obedience, God will reward. He will order your steps and will bless you beyond your petitions.

There are seasons of planting and reaping.

In those times where you are sowing by giving and serving, yet it appears as though everything you are doing doesn't seem to bring the blessings God promises in His Word, Pastor David Blunt says, "Don't be dismayed. It's your season of planting. If you stay faithful and continue to sow, in due time, you will reap a blessed harvest."

A LETTER TO HOLD AND READ IN YOUR WALK THROUGH THE VALLEY

MY PRECIOUS CHILD, I want you to hold close to your heart the words on this letter and read them whenever you feel downcast, for they will breathe life back into your spirit by reminding you that He who holds the key of life *loves you*.

My dear child, the love I give is not based on who you are, what you did, or what you could do.

My love is not measured on your abilities, your works or how perfect you think you have to be.

My love is not given according to your status, positions, or how holy and righteous you act.

In the simplest of expressions, I as Jehovah, Lord of Heaven and Earth, the love I give is solely founded on Who I Am.

Unmerited, Unconditional, Everlasting, Unlimited, and at its purest form of *love*.

I Am Agape love, manifested through true intimacy and relationship. My expression of love passes through all your human senses, and leaves you completely whole and connected to Me, your Beloved Father. My love is unlike any other, it transcends your human understanding, bringing nourishment to the core of your soul.

As your beloved, I set a protective safeguard around your life that encompasses

A love that forgives.
A love that completes.
A love that renews.
A love that accepts.
A love that never leaves.
A love that never rejects,
And
A love that never hurts.

It is I who is the embodiment and Author of Love, and I simply love you in response to My very nature. Love is the essence that makes Me the Almighty and the expression of My eminent Majesty.

I sacrificed what was most precious, My only son, so that nothing on Earth or in the Heavens can ever separate you from Who I Am, Love. Through Jesus Christ, you are forever connected to Me and to the love I freely, willingly, give to all my children.

As humans, you can't do anything to earn it, you can simply and only accept it through Jesus who died for it.

So therefore, do only what you can; obey My Word, worship Me, above all else, praise and have a heart of thanksgiving.

Let your lives be a reflection of your gratitude to the Cornerstone who is Love, and with it, voluntarily saved humanity.

You are by nature imperfect sinful human beings. You have all made mistake after mistake.

You have broken promises, and have hurt those closest to you.

You have done things you feel guilt and shame over.

You have made decisions you wish you could go back and change.

You are a fallen race, born with sin to a corrupt and polluted world.

But as God who created all things, I formed you in your mother's womb because I created what pleased me.

For even if you bare the mark of dust of the earth, and your fallen state precedes you, I love you like no other; for you are my most prized possession.

My beautiful child, always remember that my love is not conditioned on who you are, rather, in everything I Am.

Through Jesus Christ,

You are forgiven.
You are set free.
You are reborn.
You are accepted.
You belong.
You will live for eternity.
You are and will forever be with your *One True Love*.

Stage 4

Remade from Broken Pieces

You're blessed when you feel you've lost what is most dear to you.
Only then can you be embraced by the One most dear to you.
—Matthew 5:4 (MSG)

*T*IME TO STOP MOURNING

Brief Reflection

I NEVER KNEW my earthly father. The only things I have of him are my facial features, a photograph, and stories of abuse.

Growing up, I remember a deep desire to meet my father. You know, the one that's supposed to teach me how to do things like ride a bike, drive or, more importantly, protect me from those who took advantage of me. I would often have fantasies about meeting him for the first time. I tried to imagine how I would feel being held in his arms—to feel his unconditional love, to feel like no one could harm me as long as he was with me.

Year after year, I waited for him to suddenly appear so we could make up for the lost time, but it never happened. I needed my father but he wasn't there. And as a child and teenager, his absence affected me in so many ways. Looking to fill the gap he left, I tried to find love in all the wrong people which only left me emptier and feeling more insignificant.

But as I look back now, I always had someone watching over me. Unbeknownst to me, God, my creator and Heavenly Father, was always there. Looking back, I can see the countless times He kept me safe, the numerous times He protected me, and redirected my steps from the wrong direction I was heading.

No matter how many terrible decisions I made—and believe me, they were plenty—my Heavenly Father didn't give up on me. No matter how broken I was inside or how much anger and hate my heart held, He never turned his back on me. Instead, He would keep watch over me, seeing me through the sacrifice of Jesus and the loving eyes of a real Father. He often called out for me, constantly knocking at the door of my heart, waiting patiently for me to answer and open the door. He wanted me; He accepted me regardless of how messed up I was. He kept reaching out to me, never abandoning me until that day when I finally said, "Yes, Father, here I am. Please, come in."

Today, as I sit here and reflect on my past, I am amazed on what my Heavenly Father has done for me. No, I didn't have my earthly father, but my real Father was always there providing the correction, instructions, protection and, most importantly, the love I needed. I didn't know Him very well growing up. I didn't recognize His voice and, when I did, many times I rejected it; but thanks be to Jesus who is always interceding for us before the Father.

This reminds me that if He did not give up on me then, He will not give up on me now. He is my true Father. He loves me more than I can ever comprehend, so I know for certain, He will help me get through any season just like He did before.

It's Time to Stop Crying

In the book of 1 Samuel, chapter 15 and 16, we read about God's rejection of Saul as the King of Israel, due to his conscious and continual disobedience to the specific commands that the Lord had given him. In addition, we are previewed to the Prophet Samuel's emotional response to Saul's future fate and the Lord's acknowledgement.

> Then Samuel went home to Ramah, and Saul returned to his house at Gibeah of Saul. Samuel never went to meet with Saul again, but he mourned constantly for him. And the Lord

was sorry he had ever made Saul king of Israel.
(1 Samuel 15:34–35, NLT)

Then it says,

> Now the Lord said to Samuel, "You have mourned
> long enough for Saul. I have rejected him as king
> of Israel, so fill your flask with olive oil and go to
> Bethlehem. Find a man named Jesse who lives
> there, for I have selected one of his sons to be my
> king." (1 Samuel 16:1, NLT)

This part of the story stood out to me in a profound way for two reasons.

First, because Samuel mourned for Saul for a period of time; how long, the Bible does not mention. But God knew when the time for mourning was over, and He told Samuel it was time to move on.

Second, because God's will and purpose will always prevail no matter the circumstances. He allowed the Prophet Samuel to mourn for Saul for a period of time. I believe God is very much in tune with human emotions, and the need for them to be processed in order to move on. The Prophet Samuel dealt with his emotions before the Lord. I believe that it was through this intimate relationship that God knew Samuel was ready to continue on with his assignment.

Through this illustration in the Bible, we can infer that the best way to move forward after a loss is to go forth with the assignment God has entrusted each and every one of us to accomplish here on earth. It is in the pursuit and the engagement of that calling that we find true wholeness and fulfilment. It is by going out, and meeting a need that true joy is experienced.

Hence, in my own paraphrasing, God told the prophet Samuel to wipe his face, take a shower, get himself together because there's a new assignment and a need to be met. This example reflects the turning point in my process where I went from mourning to rejoicing through the act of serving, meeting a need, and continuing on my God-given assignment, and eventually, writing this very book.

Let me further explain.

For about two years, I mourned over the separation in my marriage; weeping day in and day out over all the memories we shared, and all the dreams, and goals we had as a family that now seemed to be thrown into the fire to burn without mercy until all that is left are the ashes, and smoke to remind us of what was and what is no more. Yes, that was a run on sentence, but the emotion called for it.

I had shed tears without ceasing, prayed fervently night and day, fasted to hear God's voice, sought Christian counsel, sought forgiveness and reconciliation. I did, and I did some more until I did all I knew and could do. In the beginning of my grieving process, I distanced myself from others, secluding myself to cradle and deal with my dissolution in life, but I always dealt with the raw of the pain before God—many times on the floor, crying out to Him for help and rescue, to show me what I needed to do.

And He did.

> Who are those who fear the Lord? He will show them the path they should choose. (Psalm 25:12, NLT)

How?

Well, first, He showed me through His Word.

> Then [Ezra] told them, "Go your way, eat the fat, drink the sweet drink, and send portions to him for whom nothing is prepared; for this day is holy to our Lord. And be not grieved and depressed, for the joy of the Lord is your strength and stronghold." (Nehemiah 8:10, AMPC)

He indeed was my breath of life. The only way to get up in the morning and be effective, productive, and efficient in continuing to care for my children, my household, my job, serve and lead in my church, lend a helping hand when someone needed me, care for my overall health, stay loyal and obedient to God, and walk with integrity, was only—and I mean only—by the Lord's strength and stronghold.

Through the empowerment of the Holy Spirit, I stayed connected to God, and through that connection, I received the nourishment I needed to do the very thing that would take me to the next level in my Christian walk even in the midst of a crisis—helping and serving others.

> Feed the hungry and help those in trouble. Then your light will shine out from the darkness, and the darkness around you will be as bright as noon. The Lord will guide you continually, giving you water when you are dry and restoring your strength. You will be like a well-watered garden, like an ever-flowing spring. (Isaiah 58:10–11, NLT)

In fact, during the most difficult times in my process, serving or being there for someone who needed me brought me comfort. God allowed me time to mourn, but He didn't want me to dwell there for too long or else, I would lose focus, become weak, and be an easy target for the enemy. If I continued to hang on to my loss and hold on to my pain, I would be unable to fulfil my assignment, and not fulfilling my assignment means those who are counting on my help would be at stake. So through my constant connection with the Lord, the Holy Spirit girded me with the mental, emotional, spiritual, and even physical capacity I needed to wipe my face, take a shower, get myself together, and go out and serve.

Not only did the Holy Spirit empower me to serve with the best of my ability, but He enabled me to write this book so that you, my friend, can be encouraged to do the same.

> La disposición de usar el don que tienes, en tu proceso de «cárcel», te abrirá las puertas que te conducirán a tu destino.

Translation:
> Your disposition to use the gift you have, in your process of <prison>, will open the doors that will lead you to your destiny. (Yesenia Then, *Te Desafío a Crecer*)

So where do you begin? You can start right where you are at—with your family. Then you can serve in your church, in your community, in your place of employment, with friends and neighbors, through outreach near or far; you can make a difference no matter what age, stage, or circumstance you're in today.

All you need is a willing heart, and the use of what you already have, and possess inside. Take one step outside your comfort zone, pause, take a deep breath, then in faith, take another. Trust that with each step you take, Jesus is right beside you, guiding you through this obstacle called life. You will discover, my friend, that as you walk with Jesus by your side, doors will begin to open, and even in the middle of your heartache, you will experience God's indescribable blessings.

Don't let anything or anyone prevent you from moving forward and reaching your destiny.

You are never alone.

In the book of Esther, Mordecai, Esther's cousin and guardian, sent this message to her while she was at the king's palace:

> If you keep quiet at a time like this, deliverance and relief for the Jews will arise from some other place, but you and your relatives will die. Who knows if perhaps you were made queen for just such a time as this? (Esther 4:14, NLT)

This can also be a message for you and me. God will accomplish His purpose with you or without you, for His Word will always prevail and never returns back void. But if you stay silent, if you give up, if you give into fear, depression, and despair, or if you lose yourself in grief, you will lose your blessing, the ability to go to the next level, and the fulfilment of your destiny. And like Mordecai said, "Who knows if perhaps (God allowed you to be in this position) for just such a time as this (to fulfill a God-given assignment that cannot otherwise be completed unless you or someone in your place were in that situation)?"

> For even the Son of Man came not to be served
> but to serve others and to give his life as a ransom
> for many. (Matthew 20:28, NLT)

TIME TO START LIVING

God doesn't want something from you. He wants something for you. Your value is not in what you do (as if you could ever do enough) but in who you are (as if you could ever be more loved and accepted by Him than you already are).

This, too, is what Sabbath is meant to communicate. You don't need to keep pushing, rushing, gathering, hustling. You've already received approval from the only One whose approval really matters. He has stamped His value on you, and that is enough.

Even the activities He gives you to steward are not given to see how many balls you can juggle, but instead so you can participate with Him in staking a kingdom claim on the patches of ground where you live. Sure, there's sweat involved. Sore muscles. Dirt under your pretty fingernails. But these endeavors and hobbies and accumulated possessions of yours are meant to bring joy, to enhance relationships, to develop your gifts, to swell you with His blessing and contentment. They're not supposed to be nothing but pressure. (Priscilla Shirer, *Fervent*)

MARCH 18, 2018, I turned forty years old. That morning, I was greeted with a song, a wonderful breakfast, cupcakes, a candle, presents, a big poster board with pictures, and beautiful words from my daughters.

It was almost picture perfect. I felt in that moment, I didn't need anything else for that day. But as beautiful as that morning was, there was something else that had a profound touch in my heart which, today, I feel gave me a greater push to pursue the desires God had placed in my heart.

That day at church, one of my leaders was congratulating me on my birthday and he said, "I imagine you have accomplished many things up this point." That one word—accomplished—pierced right through my heart, and I could not stop dwelling on it and what it meant at that stage in my life. For the next few days, I kept pondering on it. I began to feel extremely disappointed in myself. For as I looked at my life span, I felt as though, compared to other people, I had not accomplished much. I began to talk with God about how I was feeling, and the direction He wanted me to go and He brought to mind this verse:

> Yes, everything else is worthless when compared with the infinite value of knowing Christ Jesus my Lord. For his sake I have discarded everything else, counting it all as garbage, so that I could gain Christ and become one with him. I no longer count on my own righteousness through obeying the law; rather, I become righteous through faith in Christ. For God's way of making us right with himself depends on faith. (Philippians 3:8–9, NLT)

This verse spoke deeply to my spirit. It reminded me that many of us are walking through life with an individualized, self-seeking, self-centered, and self-focused mindset. But if we take a magnifying glass to this choice of life, we will discover that the only thing it breeds are things like selfishness, egoism, pretenses, and a lack of compassion for other people in our world. Furthermore, when no one is watching, the only company left is loneliness, emptiness, and a lack of fulfillment. Why? Because God, our creator, made us with an imprinted desire to live a life where He is at the very center of everything we do.

When we pass every decision, and every step through our communion with Jesus, we can expect to have joy when the world says we should be sad. We can expect to have peace when the world says we should be anxious. We can expect to be strong when the world says we should be weak. And we can expect to live a life of purpose when the world says it's over.

For we do not live by the world's system; we live our lives grounded in Christ Jesus. That, my friend, is where we can start living. Once we have this at the core of our hearts, everything else will fall in place.

> Life isn't about what we produce but who we become. (Tiffany Bluhm)

When you come to grips with the fact that life is not about you, you are able to depose unnecessary weight off your shoulders and let go of unrealistic expectations. You'll find yourself taking more risks, doing things out of your comfort zone (like flying on an airplane without your family for the first time, to go to a country you have never been, on a mission trip, to do something you've never done like build a house). You'll find yourself looking for opportunities to put a smile on someone's face, moments to pay it forward, possibilities to leave a lasting mark on this world. And in those times when you feel alone, instead of feeling unloved, sad, and incomplete, you'll find yourself enjoying your own company, in connection with God's presence; doing things that add value to your life and those you were called to impact.

You see, my friend, the enemy came full force against me and tried to debilitate me through the separation with my husband; but because he didn't know the essence within me, what he actually did was propel me closer to Jesus. This allowed God to use my brokenness to bring out my true identity, and turn things around for my good. One of the most remarkable ways He did this was by giving me one of my heart's desire—one that aligned with His will for my life.

I want to share with you all one the most wonderful gift experience God granted me, one that was embedded in my heart for a very long time—the privilege to go on a missions trip. It's the journey that ignited my passion and calling to help the brokenhearted. And I hope you don't mind me sharing how it marked my life, for I believe it will inspire you to start living the life God has called you to live.

There we were eleven individuals from different stages, ages, and cultural backgrounds coming together for one purpose—to make a lasting difference. But what we didn't know was how our lives would forever be impacted.

One of the most significant moments of the mission trip was the last day when the bus driver taking us back to the airport, stood up, and said these words; "There are pleasures of the body, such as eating, and sleeping. There are pleasures of the heart. For instance, say, I give something to someone and they give me a gift back. Then there are pleasures of the spirit where you give something to someone who can't give you nothing back. That act, when what we do for someone else can't be repaid, is what makes the spirit within us truly happy. It's the moment where we feel genuinely fulfilled." He went on to say that our group did not just come to Guatemala to build a house for a family who desperately needed it, we were actually leaving the country having left our footprints on the earth. At that moment, I believe we were all stunned by the words of wisdom this man had just deposited into our hearts, right before our departure back to what awaited each of us back home. Words that still ring clear in my mind: *I left my footprint in the lives of a beautiful family of five, and in their beautiful country through the house I helped build for them.* I say, my spirit had never been fuller.

There we were, a small group from Church on the Rock, going to a country we had never been before with people we barely knew, to build a house most of us had no clue how to do. For me, it was the best way to reset my mind, start a new page in my life, and start living again. Only this time, it would be for the service of others.

When I close my eyes, I can still see the images of a team who worked hard with excellence, who were motivated by a Jesus kind of love, who developed a bond as a group, and the families that were forged by the teachings of loving pastors (David and Kim Blunt).

Every cement mixture, every measurement, every nail hammered, every wall put up, every window installed, every room wired; every drop of sweat, every frustration, every ache, every thirst, every hunger; every laughter, every hug, every accomplishment, every lesson, every eye connection, every game with the children, every picture, every time we sat down to a delicious lunch with the families, and with each other; every tear, every heartache; every morning waking up to birthday fireworks, and the crows singing; the serenity of the morning, sunset, the cool of the evening; the nightly devotions where hearts were opened and tears were shed; the games that made us laugh, jump, and fall down; the God encounters, the whispers of the Holy Spirit, the sharpening of our gifting, the confirmations of God's calling in our lives—these brought change. In the words of one of the group members, "We went there to change a family's life, but in turn, they changed ours." My heart still yearns to be present again in that time, that place, with that team, where all that mattered was what we could give and do for someone else.

On this trip to Guatemala, I discovered that God is very attuned to our heart's desires, and gives them to us in perfect timing. I learned not only to hammer in nails to put together panels and make a wall or how to do a cement mix, but the Holy Spirit confirmed the gifts He has given me, and my calling to serve, help, and encourage others.

This trip changed my life in such a way that I can only describe it in the words of our "Casas Por Cristo" intern in Guatemala, when he said one night during our devotional meetings, "Life is a moment," which my heart translated to mean: "Live in the moment, Denise, for you may have today, but tomorrow is not promised. Make certain to make a difference everywhere you go, and with every chance you are granted. Don't get so caught up in the busyness of life that you miss out on life's beautiful moments—moments that are here today and gone tomorrow. Take time to savor and cherish the life you have been given, and use it to impact the world around you. With little or with much, use what you've got to bring hope to hurting."

My friends, I share this extraordinary experience with you all because I believe God is calling you to *start* living a life where you are no longer a bystander. A life where your gifting is being used to its highest potential as you meet needs and change lives with the love of Christ. The *time* has come for you to adhere to the call on your life. Stop waiting for things to change; become the change.

And yes, I strongly encourage you to go on a mission's trip. It will transform your life, one way or another.

TAKE GOOD CARE OF YOUR BODY, SOUL AND SPIRIT (BSS)

DURING SEASONS OF crisis, many of us give in to the tendency of neglecting our overall health. We focus on all that is happening to us and forget about all the damage we are causing within ourselves.

For me, the well-being of my body, soul and spirit was important, not just because my two girls depended on me, but the Holy Spirit depended on my health in order to use me without restrictions.

What kept me in tune with wanting to keep myself healthy, and not look on the outside like a train came crashing through my life (which was how I felt inside) was first understanding who I was, who I belong to and represented—God.

> "Men and women of faith do not live trouble-free lives, they live by faith in the midst of troubling times and circumstances." (By Ken Blanchard)

It was more important for me to live out my faith during those times of difficulty than in the days of joy. Because it's during those times when everything in your life is coming undone, that your faith is put to the test, and when most people are watching to see if what you believe is authentic. It was, and it is, very important for me to walk with integrity to what I speak, and the convictions I stand on. I can't speak of a God who is for me, if I am walking around neglecting my overall health; including His temple.

> Comprehending, when we give our lives to Jesus, we no longer live for ourselves, that our bodies are not our own, is the foundation to leading a healthy lifestyle even under fire. Jesus Christ sacrificed His life for each and one of us, and when we invite Him into our hearts, the Holy Spirit takes residence in us, and it's our responsibility to make sure we take great care of it inside and out. God hasn't invited us into a disorderly, unkempt life but into something holy and beautiful—as beautiful on the inside as the outside. (1 Thessalonians 4:6–7, MSG)

Taking care of ourselves is not about measuring up to anything or anyone. It's not about a number on a scale or having the body of an airbrushed model, rather, it is about loving God and loving yourself. This combination of love will drive you to do your very best to take care of God's house—your body, your soul, and your spirit. I believe that God can do more with our lives if we maintain a healthy lifestyle.

> A calm and undisturbed mind and heart are the life and health of the body, but envy, jealousy, and wrath are like rottenness of the bones. (Proverbs 14:30, AMPC)

This verse teaches us that our thoughts, and emotions influence the health condition of our bodies. A mind full of toxic thoughts, a heart full of offense, and a spirit disconnected from the Lord "are like rottenness of the bones."

There were times during my most sorrowful days that I would speak to a friend, and they could not understand how I had the strength to fix myself up, have a smile on my face, and still have the ability to be there for others. I would always say that it was not by my strength, but by the Spirit who lives in me. The Holy Spirit would help me get up every morning and get ready, because, my friend, there were many days—and I mean, many— I solely operated on His power. I wanted God to be glorified, and His power to be displayed through my weakness.

I remember the days when I would take a shower to drown out the despair in my cries or sitting in front on my vanity putting on my makeup, and tears would swell up as I tried hard to get ready for work. I remember not having the strength to even put my clothes on. But without fail, the Holy Spirit would whisper within me, *"Denise, you can do this. You will get through this. You will overcome this. Denise, you are going to be all right. You are not alone. I am here with you. I will help you one step at a time, one day at a time. Just breathe and release your grip. Let me take control."*

There were times I felt so torn apart, I had to shower and get dressed in the dark. But no matter how distraught I felt, the Holy Spirit pushed me forward. He didn't let me give into depression long enough for it to take up residence there. He kept reminding me of who I was, who I belong to, and who I represented—the Trinity.

To have a "calm and undisturbed mind" allows us to care for our well-being, but how do we get there when things in our lives are flipped upside down? Again, by remembering *who* we are and *whose* we are. When our worth and identity is not grounded in people or things but in Jesus, we are able to take great care of our inner and outer selves.

> So then, whether you eat or drink, or whatever
> you may do, do all for the honor and glory of
> God. (1 Corinthians 10:31, AMPC)

One day, I was speaking to a gentleman from my home church, and we were talking about being mindful with our health. He said something that, until this day, has stuck with me, "I eat for performance." In others words, he explained that he was very careful to eat only the foods that brought the right nutrition to his body so that he can perform at a higher level. It took time and research. And with the help of the Holy Spirit and a nutritionist, he learned to better care for his overall health.

As I had gotten older, I've noticed that my body does not function as it did in my younger years, especially when it comes to weight, energy, and even the kinds of food my body tolerates.

Now having taken time to pay attention to what my body tells me, and how it feels, and reacts to certain foods, I realized that there are foods that were not only depleting my energy, but causing a ruckus in my stomach. I had to make a decision to limit and, in some cases, eliminate foods I loved to eat for the sake of the health and performance of my body.

I purposely avoid buying junk food as much as I can with kids, and buy healthier options in order to avoid the temptation of indulgence. I put on my Fitbit, and I set a daily goal. Even when I am at work, the students know that when I go outside on a break, I am on a mission to get my steps in.

I also realized that I needed people to hold me accountable, be supportive, and who would encourage me to stay focused. So I got together with a few of my closest church family who had the same interest, and we started a health group. We shared healthy recipes, daily encouragements, exercise videos, ideas, and we also got together to workout, and keep each other motivated. So if you feel stuck, and don't know where to begin, ask a friend to join you.

> As iron sharpens iron, so a friend sharpens a friend. (Proverbs 27:17, NLT)

In an article from *Harvard Health Publishing* called "Exercise Is an All-Natural Treatment to Fight Depression," they discussed how exercise can serve as antidepressant. When you exercise, your body "releases the body's feel-good chemicals called endorphins." In addition, doing "low-intensity exercise sustained over time, releases proteins called neurotrophic or growth factors, which cause nerve cells to grow and make new connections. The improvement of brain function makes you feel better."

Maybe you feel so depressed the last thing you have a desire to do is exercise, or maybe you just don't know where to start. My personal encouragement is to start with walking. I prefer to walk because I can clear my mind, talk to God, and be active all at the same time. I can appreciate all the beauty that surrounds me, and I even meet new people. No matter what form of activity you choose, focus on the benefit to your overall health.

The motto that I have adopted for the sake of my own well-being is: "Eat and live for purpose, not indulgence." What is the purpose, you ask? To have energy, stamina, mental alertness, agility, endurance, strength, and an overall healthy BSS.

The soul is so powerful that it influences the way we feel physically.

Toxic chemicals released in our bodies due to negative thoughts can weaken our bodies.

This a strategic plan the enemy uses to hinder our performance. He does not want us to live out our personal best. He wants us to major in the minors to keep us at a level he can control.

So what do we do?

We must meet him at the battle of our soul.

We need to flush out everything contrary to God's truth.

We must tear down the beaver dam created by negative strongholds in our minds, and let the blood of Jesus Christ be released through our soul like a mighty flood.

One of the ways I keep a healthy mind is my love for reading. I read and study the Bible. I read devotionals and, at least, one new book a month. And not just any book. I don't read for entertainment; I prefer books that help me grow personally. This keeps my mind healthy.

And my spirit is healthy when I make small talk with the Lord throughout my day, no matter what I am doing.

Does this mean I have it all together, that I never get negative or have a bad day, that I always eat healthy and never eat a burger and fries? Absolutely not. I do and I do. What I'm simply saying is that your body will thank you when you eat those delicious foods, on occasion. And that when you let the negativity in your mind lead your responses in life and you slip (and we all do), we have direct access to Jesus and the Holy Spirit our Helper.

God has given us the ability to choose from good and evil, and He encourages us to never get tired of doing good. To choose to "fix your thoughts on what is true, and honorable, and right, and pure, and lovely, and admirable. Think about things that are excellent and worthy of praise" (Philippians 4:8, NLT).

Taking care of my health—my *body, soul* and *spirit* (BSS)—helped me not give into unhealthy alternatives to falsely ease my pain during my crisis.

You are God's workmanship, and you must believe that in your core. It's important to have a healthy outlook on oneself because how you view the person you are on the inside and outside will also exemplify the God who lives in you.

If you're unsatisfied with the state of your BSS, ask the Holy Spirit to help you. Ask Him to help you love yourself; to be comfortable in who God made you; to heal your mind and your emotions; to help you make better choices about the foods you eat, the activities you engage in, and how to better care for His temple.

Take inventory of what you allow to come in and out of your life, the way in which you present yourself, and ask God what areas need your attention.

You are beautiful/handsome, and no matter what you are going through today, do your best to let your light shine.

> As a Christian, God calls you to be consecrated, set-apart, and dedicated to the Lord, to honor Him with every facet of your life—including your body." (Elizabeth George)

FRIENDS TO LEAN ON

As iron sharpens iron, so a friend sharpens a
friend. (Proverbs 27:17, NLT)

THOSE WHO KNOW me, know that I am a private person. I try
to be very careful about who I confide in about personal matters.

I have learned the hard way through past experiences that not
everyone has the capacity to handle with care other people's hearts
during a crisis. When we are distraught and so desperate for answers,
often, we make the mistake of sharing our pain with individuals who
do not have our best interest in mind or don't possess the spiritual
maturity to impart wisdom into our lives.

The wrong people can use your trust and turn it against you or
use it as a form of entertainment with others by twisting, and making your story their own version of it. Other times, they simply turn
their backs on you because you are no longer of use to them or you
no longer fit their status.

That's why, one of my biggest encouragements is to make sure
that your confidant and greatest friend is Jesus. He is the only one
who will never ever let you down. He is there when others turn their
backs, leave, reject, or gossip about you. He is the friend that sticks
closer than a brother.

Jesus will always be your most loyal, faithful friend, so before you go to anyone else for counsel, be sure to bring your troubles and questions to Him first. He will then take care of bringing you the support you need from individuals who truly love and care about you.

That is what He did for me.

During the beginning season of my very painful process, I sought God earnestly and fervently. It was He and I from the start. But He knew that I needed support from individuals who would listen, pray, and stand with me through my darkest hours. I was very hesitant at first, but deep down, I knew I had to trust someone, because I could not go through the breaking process alone. I had to let go of the fear of being judged or criticized or looked upon differently.

I was able to do that when I learned to see myself through the eyes of love, mercy, grace, and compassion of Jesus Christ. His acceptance gave me the freedom to be okay, regardless of what others thought about me. Because as long as Jesus loves me, that is all that truly matters.

And it was that unconditional love that He has for me that brought to my life friends who became closer than family; friends who cried with me, who stood by me and encouraged me in the Lord when I needed strength. These were friends that didn't need to know all the details about my situation; for them it was about lifting my hands up when I was too weak to lift them up for myself.

> A friend is always loyal, and a brother is born to
> help in time of need. (Proverbs 17:17, NLT)

I truly believe this was God's way of assuring me that He was with me, that He is for me, and that He will never abandon me.

In her book, *Broken Heart on Hold: Surviving Separation*, Linda Rooks makes reference to "whom to trust at this vulnerable point in your life; your primary concern needs to be how a confidant's reactions, advice, and responses will affect your heart. Does the person have wisdom? Does she share your principles? Can she offer God's perspective?"

This is very important when sharing your heart; you want to steer away from counsel that does not align itself with the Word of God. A good way to know is if it brings you inward peace.

Linda Rooks goes on to say that, "A wise friend will allow you to pour out your heart and listen before jumping to conclusions and offering advice. And when she does make suggestions, her words will encourage, inspire, challenge, and comfort."

> Two people are better off than one, for they can help each other succeed. If one person falls, the other can reach out and help. But someone who falls alone is in real trouble. (Ecclesiastes 4:9–10, NLT)

If you have found yourself in a tough situation, and you don't know what to do or who to ask for help, I would highly suggest you run to Jesus first. There is no better friend than the One who gave His life for you and I.

Be mindful that there'll be people who you considered friends that will suddenly stop associating themselves with you, people who will barely speak to you, who will look the another way when they see you coming or ask how you are doing out of pity. But instead of feeling sad, rejoice. YES, I said REJOICE. Why? It is during the days of trouble that we discover the people who are truly for us. It's during stormy seasons where the wheat is separated from the grains. So in the words of Pastor TD Jakes, "If people in your life are willing to walk away, then LET THEM GO." They are no longer meant to be a part of your journey.

Then ask the Lord to surround you with individuals who will stand by you through the good and the ugly, individuals who are for you, who are able to give you Godly counsel, and the help you need to get through your season.

5 The Keys to Overcome, Grow, and Live Free

You are an overcomer when nothing you have
faced in life defines you but God.
You grow when you can look at your mishaps and mistakes,
and instead of being a victim, you decide to learn from them.
You live free when the opinion of others are
not the factors for your self-worth.
You are an overcomer, a person of growth, and you live in
freedom when God's Word is your guide, prayer is your
sustenance, the Lord is your mediator, and joy is your reward.
—Denise Riaño

$\mathcal{S}$TAY CONNECTED TO THE VINE

Thank God Elijah was "a human being, even as we are" [James 5:17]! He sat under a tree, complained to God and expressed his unbelief—just as we have often done. Yet this was not the case at all when he was truly in touch with God. "Elijah was a human being, even as we are," yet "he prayed earnestly." The literal meaning of this in the Greek is magnificent: Instead of saying, "earnestly," it says, "He prayed in prayer." In other words, "He kept on praying." The lesson here is that you must keep praying.

After Elijah had called down fire from heaven to defeat the prophets of Baal, rain was needed for God's prophecy to be fulfilled...We are told, "Elijah...bent down to the ground and put his face between his knees" (1 Kings 18:42), shutting out all sights and sounds. He put himself in a position, beneath his robe, to neither see nor hear what was happening.

Elijah then said to his servant, "Go and look toward the sea" (1 Kings 18:43). Upon returning, the servant replied, "There is nothing there"...

Can you imagine what we would do under the same circumstances?…But did Elijah give up? No. In fact, six times he told his servant, "Go back." Each time the servant returned saying, "Nothing!"

Yet "the seventh time the servant reported, 'A cloud as small as a man's hand is rising from the sea'" (1 Kings 18:44)…And the rains came… fast, and furiously…Yes, in spite of utterly hopeless reports received from sight, this is a story of faith that continues "praying in prayer."

Do you know how to pray in that way— how to prevail in prayer? Let your sight bring you reports as discouraging as possible, but pay no attention to them. Our heavenly Father lives, and even the delays of answers to our prayers are part of his goodness. (Arthur Tappan Pierson, *Streams in the Desert* devotional)

I CAN REMEMBER the numerous times, I was at work, looking forward to lunch or a small break in between to share my heart with my Heavenly Father. While my lunch would refuel my body, my communion with God would refuel my spirit.

Constant communication with God is, literally, the key to living at peace especially during a life crisis. I have learned to be unmovable in my faith through communion with God no matter what I am doing.

I can recall, oftentimes, lying awake in my bed under the covers, praying in a soft whisper, "Father, please hold my heart." I could see the image of me handing over my heart to him, and seeing him cover it with His hands. I would ask Him to heal my broken pieces; to come close to me, to overwhelm me with His embrace, and love me until all pain was gone; to hold me until I fell fast asleep. Sometimes it was around one o'clock in the morning and other times were three o'clock or five o'clock in the morning. I'd sit up in my bed and simply ask God to show me what to do. I would pray in the shower, while cleaning, while cooking, while driving—every day, at every chance I got.

> Evening, and morning, and at noon, will I pray, and cry aloud: and he shall hear my voice. (Psalms 55:17, KJV)

The simple prayers that, many times, I barely uttered were the most profound. It allowed God to just hold and comfort me.

My dear friend, there'll be days when you will feel so pressed with deep sadness, and so fragile in body that your mouth will find it challenging to open. No worries, you have help. You have an intimate friend who will pray for you.

> So too the [Holy] Spirit comes to our aid and bears us up in our weakness; for we do not know what prayer to offer nor how to offer it worthily as we ought, but the Spirit Himself goes to meet our supplication and pleads in our behalf with unspeakable yearnings and groanings too deep for utterance. And He Who searches the hearts of men knows what is in the mind of the [Holy] Spirit [what His intent is], because the Spirit intercedes and pleads [before God] in behalf of the saints according to and in harmony with God's will. [Ps. 139:1, 2.]

(Romans 8:26–27, AMPC)

So when you are unable to formulate words to pray, let the Spirit of God pray and intercede for you. And if you don't know how, just ask Him to show you, and He will.

In her book, *Life Management for Busy Women*, Elizabeth George says that "through prayer, you open up your heart to God. And when you do, He searches it, draws out your motives, and offers you the opportunity to bring your will into alignment with His plan."

I have learned from this process that when you are faced with life challenges, to effectively allow God to work out His plan in your life, maintaining constant communication with Him is vital. So even when my flesh wanted to distance itself from God, I would allow His Spirit to lead me to just sit in His presence or open up the Bible and pray His Word. I would go to the Book of Psalms because David was a man who was able to express his internal agony and still worship and trust God.

> Those who look to him for help will be radiant with joy; no shadow of shame will darken their faces. In my desperation I prayed, and the Lord listened; he saved me from all my troubles. For the angel of the Lord is a guard; he surrounds and defends all who fear him. (Psalm 34:5–7, NLT)

There will be moments in your walk with God when you, too, will feel discouraged, and you are not going to feel like praying. There will be times where you will feel so troubled by your circumstance that the only thing you want to do is go under the covers, talk to no one, and just sleep. But as bad as you want to do that, do yourself a favor, and don't. Because that's exactly what Satan wants you to do; he wants you disconnected from God, from those who care about you, and steal your blessings.

> Intentionally positioning yourself under God's directive leadership is the only way to know you are in the right place to receive his guidance in every aspect of your life. (Kannetra A. Bryant, EdD)

So, my friend, you must push and push through. Come on, push. You can do it. Get up and move past those emotions and seek the Lord; He is waiting.

The Word of God says that there is nothing too small, too big that we can't bring to God. He loves us so much; He wants us to come to him about everything. If all you have is tears then cry before Him, lay your burdens at the feet of Jesus. Grab on to His hem; it has the power to make beauty out of ashes.

Make a personal commitment to purposely go before God throughout your day, every day, even if you have to drag yourself there. No matter what, *just do it.*

For years, I have had the privilege of being a part of a prayer line called W.H.I.P (Women Hallowed In Prayer) ministry. A group of four women come together over the phone at the same time, once a week, in different parts of the world, and we pray for one another. Being a part of this prayer ministry with my group of ladies has been a tremendous blessing. I know I can count on them to lift me up when I can't do it for myself. When we are crushed in spirit, we have each other's back as prayer intercessors.

I encourage you to find, join, or create a prayer group that will kneel with you, and lift your weary heart to God by way of support and intercession.

> Yes, I am the vine; you are the branches. Those who remain in me, and I in them, will produce much fruit. For apart from me you can do nothing. Anyone who does not remain in me is thrown away like a useless branch and withers. Such branches are gathered into a pile to be burned. But if you remain in me and my words remain in you, you may ask for anything you want, and it will be granted! When you produce much fruit, you are my true disciples. This brings great glory to my Father. (John 15:5–8, NLT)

We must remain in Him, regardless of what comes our way via our own doing, Satan's, or the Lord's; it's the only way to continue to grow, produce, and not wither away.

Our intimate communion with our Lord gives clarity to the confusing areas of our lives. And as we patiently wait on Him, He will deposit the answers to our desperate questions. He gives us a boost of strength to put one foot in front of the other and not fall. Being connected to God is how we are able to see the light to our path so we don't trip and make the wrong decisions. Our union with Him gives us the power to spread our wings like eagles and soar above our circumstances. But we must commune, stay joined to Him, no matter what, every day, at every chance we get.

There is a life-producing nourishment that flows from the Vine (God) to the branch (His children) that allows for blessings, miracles, and breakthroughs to manifest. Staying attached is what allows us to produce that which gives life to a dying world.

Don't let anything that happens in your life disconnect you from the Vine, the Lord Jesus Christ, for He alone is the giver of life even after death.

*L*IFE'S GPS

HAVE YOU EVER been lost? I mean, really lost to the point you were scared half to death? Have you ever found yourself driving along a road going in the direction that was customary in your daily routine, so much so that, sometimes, you would arrive at your destination and you don't know how you got there? But on one particular day, as you were driving in your accustomed route, suddenly, you realized that you were in the wrong place and in an area that seemed to lead to a dead end. Your heart started beating fast, your hands began to shake, your breathing became heavy, your body got hot, and tears were not far behind—all because you found yourself in an unknown place—and in that moment, scared and simply clueless as how to find your way back.

That, my friend, is where I found myself in my family crisis—completely lost, afraid, and clueless of what to do. At first, I tried to find my own way out, but all I did was get myself even more lost. But thankfully, I had something that became my saving grace, my rescue and guide to finding my way back and follow the right path—the Word of God. The Bible became my internal GPS. It was one of the lifelines that helped me find hope again.

You have probably heard from your Pastor, or some other source that you should read and follow God's Word. My purpose with this chapter is to give you an illustration through my own life experience as to why soaking yourself in the Word of God is the most powerful tool, and weapon you will ever need for every season and every occasion in your life.

> Such things were written in the Scriptures long ago to teach us. And the Scriptures give us hope and encouragement as we wait patiently for God's promises to be fulfilled. (Romans 15:4, NLT)
>
> Study this Book of Instruction continually. Meditate on it day and night so you will be sure to obey everything written in it. Only then will you prosper and succeed in all you do. (Joshua 1:8, NLT)
>
> Every Scripture is God-breathed (given by His inspiration) and profitable for instruction, for reproof and conviction of sin, for correction of error and discipline in obedience, [and] for training in righteousness (in holy living, in conformity to God's will in thought, purpose, and action), so that the man of God may be complete and proficient, well fitted and thoroughly equipped for every good work. (2 Timothy 3:16–17, AMPC)

In my season of breaking and transformation, the Word of God became more important than food itself. The more I read it, the more my spirit craved it, needed it, and desired it. Even on my worst or busiest days, I found myself seeking it as a symbol of my stronghold. The very thing that, without a shadow of doubt, I could depend on for truth, wisdom, knowledge, and guidance. I kept a journal and pen with me, and I read, studied, and wrote the treasures the Holy Spirit deposited into my heart. The more I sought God in His Word, the more I discovered who He is, and in turn, I discovered who I was, and all that I have been graciously given through Jesus Christ.

Every time I felt unbalanced, I read the Word of God. It had the power to place my feet on the firm footing of faith. I felt stronger and

TEARS IN THE CLOSET

unmovable, regardless of who had rejected me or turned their backs on me or spoke ill of me. His Word brought freedom and healing to my hurting heart.

As a woman, I know first hand the complexity of our God given design. Our creator gave us the natural ability to birth life not just for procreation, but also in whatever we put our hands on. We have that ability to make lemonade out lemons, a delicious meal out of white rice and corned beef, and turn a run down shack into a cozy home. We can multitask diverse roles and daily responsibilities, and when life suddenly sends us on an unexpected path, we do what we know best—we keep moving. Nevertheless, as beautifully complex as we may be, there are times that even while we are moving, our movements are emotionally driven and lacking in wisdom.

So how do we move forward in an unknown road and find the path that will lead us back to our purpose? We need the life giving power, nourishment, teachings, guidance, and correction of the Word of God. There's no other way—*none*.

> But don't let it faze you. Stick with what you learned and believed, sure of the integrity of your teachers—why, you took in the sacred Scriptures with your mother's milk! There's nothing like the written word of God for showing you the way to salvation through faith in Christ Jesus. Every part of Scripture is God-breathed and useful one way or another—showing us truth, exposing our rebellion, correcting our mistakes, training us to live God's way. Through the word we are put together and shaped up for the tasks God has for us. (2 Timothy 3:14–17, MSG)

My friend, for His Word to have a powerful impact in your life, don't just read it occasionally or merely listen to it on your app or read it and forget what you've read. You must go a step further; study it, savor it, bathe in it, memorize it, and allow it to completely overtake your heart. It is your weapon against the enemy, it's your resuscitation when you've been beaten down, it's your reminder when all else fails, it's your hope in a hopeless situation, it's what gives you breath when your heart stops beating.

> What I have discovered is that only the Holy Spirit makes the Scripture come alive in my heart. Through His guidance, the Bible becomes much more than mere words—it becomes the very substance of life. (John Bevere, *The Holy Spirit*, p. 82)

My friend, if you have found yourself in a dead end, my biggest encouragement to you is don't panic, take a deep breath, and open the Word of God; The Bible.

> "When he sits on the throne as king, he must copy for himself this body of instruction on a scroll in the presence of the Levitical priests. He must always keep that copy with him and read it daily as long as he lives. That way he will learn to fear the Lord his God by obeying all the terms of these instructions and decrees. This regular reading will prevent him from becoming proud and acting as if he is above his fellow citizens. It will also prevent him from turning away from these commands in the smallest way. And it will ensure that he and his descendants will reign for many generations in Israel. (Deuteronomy 17:18–20, NLT)

Elizabeth George says, "Be a woman of one book." I love to read. I purposely read at least one new book every month. I enjoy reading leadership, and self empowerment books because they are great tools for personal growth, yet there's no book more important in my life than the Bible. If I can only read one thing, it must and should be the Bible; Without it, I feel like I'm driving to an unknown destination without a map. The Bible is what directs our life. Without constant devotion to it, there's a greater chance of taking a wrong turn. And believe me, I have, more than once, and the consequences were always regrettable. In this journey, I'm more diligent about not going a day without getting into the Word of God, and writing in a journal what touches my spirit.

God is an immeasurable God, He's more than the words in the Bible, but It is the compass He left to help us navigate successfully through this world. He constantly reminds us to carefully obey it, and never stray from it. If we are careful to follow His instructions, He will bless and show us which way to go.

> The godly offer good counsel; they teach right from wrong. They have made God's law their own, so they will never slip from his path. (Psalm 37:30–31, NLT)

I recall the early days of my gut-wrenching process when God took my heart in His hands, and like a Potter, began to take out the lumps that prevented me from displaying who I truly was. I am not going to sugar coated, it was a very grievous and lonely time for me. It was as if I had to learn how to be a new person with a new identity; something totally different than who I had been for the last 20 years.

Even though this transformation was traumatic; nevertheless, God always made sure, I had what I needed to get through victoriously—His Spirit and His Word. A few of the practical things I did to keep my focus on God's Word was displaying scripture verses on various places in my home, such as my closet, bedroom, bathroom, vanity, and my car.

I would look in the mirror and speak the Word of God to myself out loud, and believe or not, it gave me what I needed to get through the unset of my new beginning.

> The Lord himself will fight for you. Just stay calm. (Exodus 14:14, NLT)

The more I did it, the more I believed it and the more grounded I was in my faith.

On days I wanted to give up, and I thought I had no more to give, God would remind me that He wouldn't put more on me than I could handle. That there was nothing in my life He was not aware of, and I needed to trust He was in control.

> You're blessed when you stay on course, walking steadily on the road revealed by God. You're blessed when you follow his directions, doing your best to find him. That's right—you don't go off on your own; you walk straight along the road he set. You, God, prescribed the right way to live; now you expect us to live it. Oh, that my steps might be steady, keeping to the course you set; Then I'd never have any regrets in comparing my life with your counsel. I thank you for speaking straight from your heart; I learn the pattern of your righteous ways. I'm going to do what you tell me to do; don't ever walk off and leave me. How can a young person live a clean life? By carefully reading the map of your Word. I'm single-minded in pursuit of you; don't let me miss the road signs you've posted. I've banked your promises in the vault of my heart so I won't sin myself bankrupt. Be blessed, God; train me in your ways of wise living. I'll transfer to my lips all the counsel that comes from your mouth; I delight far more in what you tell me about living than in gathering a pile of riches. I ponder every morsel of wisdom from you, I attentively watch how you've done it. I relish everything you've told me of life, I won't forget a word of it. (Psalm 119:1–16, MSG

$\mathscr{F}$LESH UNDER CONTROL

I DON'T KNOW about you, but my flesh is very demanding. It seems like it always wants or needs something. I became sick and tired of my flesh dominating my thoughts, emotions, and actions.

I wanted to be able to give the Holy Spirit full access, full dominion over my whole being. I was hungry for a deeper closeness with the Lord. I had to figure out a way to stop my flesh from bullying me around and put it under control. After sharing my frustration with my best friend, the Holy Spirit, He whispered, "*Fasting.*"

I confess that before I had entered into this stormy season, I would Fast only on occasions, and most of the time, it would be corporately with my church. The twenty-one-day corporate Fasting helped jumpstart my knowledge of the breakthroughs that occur in the soul, spirit, and even the body, when our flesh is denied something it wants and enjoys.

One of the things the Holy Spirit began to show me were the things that hindered my walk with the Lord. These experiences allowed me to notice how Fasting was a way to deprive the flesh while feeding the spirit. The more I Fasted, the more the Holy Spirit was able to reveal what I needed to stop reading, watching, listening and engaging in—things that were not allowing me to go to the next level in my walk with Christ.

[Rather] is not this the fast that I have chosen: to loose the bonds of wickedness, to undo the bands of the yoke, to let the oppressed go free, and that you break every [enslaving] yoke? [Acts 8:23.] Is it not to divide your bread with the hungry and bring the homeless poor into your house—when you see the naked, that you cover him, and that you hide not yourself from [the needs of] your own flesh and blood? Then shall your light break forth like the morning, and your healing (your restoration and the power of a new life) shall spring forth speedily; your righteousness (your rightness, your justice, and your right relationship with God) shall go before you [conducting you to peace and prosperity], and the glory of the Lord shall be your rear guard. [Exod. 14:19, 20; Isa. 52:12.] Then you shall call, and the Lord will answer; you shall cry, and He will say, "Here I am." If you take away from your midst yokes of oppression [wherever you find them], the finger pointed in scorn [toward the oppressed or the godly], and every form of false, harsh, unjust, and wicked speaking, [Exod. 3:14.] And if you pour out that with which you sustain your own life for the hungry and satisfy the need of the afflicted, then shall your light rise in darkness, and your obscurity and gloom become like the noonday. And the Lord shall guide you continually and satisfy you in drought and in dry places and make strong your bones. And you shall be like a watered garden and like a spring of water whose waters fail not. (Isaiah 58:6–11, AMPC)

I wasn't trying to become religious or antiquated; I just began to crave a deeper desire to be with God. The things that I formally enjoyed no longer held my attention. The more I sought God, the more respect I had for the Holy Spirit and for things I allowed myself to entertain.

Fasting is the gateway for removing the debris from our eyes and ears. It's the act that releases us from the attachment of bad habits, and attitudes that prevent the Holy Spirit from using us to our full capacity. Fasting brings our flesh to a humble submission. It removes pride and prevents our flesh to follow its own desire.

If you are encountering a difficulty in your life, I encourage you to set aside time to Fast. Why? Fasting has a way of shutting the mouth of our flesh and allowing the Spirit to speak into our lives.

> Then I proclaimed a fast there, at the river Ahava, that we might humble ourselves before our God to seek from Him a straight and right way for us, our little ones, and all our possessions. For I was ashamed to request of the king a band of soldiers and horsemen to protect us against the enemy along the way, because we had told the king, the hand of our God is upon all them for good who seek Him, but His power and His wrath are against all those who forsake Him. So we fasted and besought our God for this, and He heard our entreaty. (Ezra 8:21–23, AMPC)

NO MORE CONDEMNATION

PRISON WAS MY home for many years. I still remember it clear-ly—a dark, gloomy room with no one in sight. Each day I cried out, screaming for help, hoping someone would hear my desperate plead-ings, but no person ever came. I tried to escape many times with my own strength, but each time, my attempts failed. You see, my friend, this was no ordinary prison where people who break the law are placed for a period of time depending on their crime. No, my prison was in my mind. Each mental prison bar was a stronghold craftily built by the enemy since my childhood. Each one represented *abandonment, rejection, low self-esteem, shame, guilt, abuse, neglect, insecurity, being an outcast, anger, bitterness, unforgiveness*, and *fear*. But the one that held the key to the prison door was *condemnation*. It taunted me daily with everything that made me feel worthless, unloved, and unwanted. This was my life for many years, until I discovered a way out—the only way out—through Jesus Christ. He told me this:

> "So now there is no condemnation for those who belong to Christ Jesus. And because you belong to him, the power of the life-giving Spirit has freed you from the power of sin that leads to death. The law of Moses was unable to save us because of the weakness of our sinful nature. So God did

what the law could not do. He sent his own Son in a body like the bodies we sinners have. And in that body God declared an end to sin's control over us by giving his Son as a sacrifice for our sins. He did this so that the just requirement of the law would be fully satisfied for us, who no longer follow our sinful nature but instead follow the Spirit. (Romans 8:1–4, NLT)

But the Lord will redeem those who serve him. No one who takes refuge in him will be condemned. (Psalms 34:22, NLT)

I had enough of the enemy's mental abuse, instead of trying to escape my mental prison with my own abilities, I called on and surrendered completely to Jesus Christ. He lovingly and compassionately set me free.

My friend, not only did He break my bondage, He destroyed each and every bar that held me captive for all those years.

"I have loved you even as the Father has loved me. Remain in my love. When you obey my commandments, you remain in my love, just as I obey my Father's commandments and remain in his love. I have told you these things so that you will be filled with my joy. Yes, your joy will overflow! This is my commandment: Love each other in the same way I have loved you. There is no greater love than to lay down one's life for one's friends. You are my friends if you do what I command. I no longer call you slaves, because a master doesn't confide in his slaves. Now you are my friends, since I have told you everything the Father told me. You didn't choose me. I chose you. I appointed you to go and produce lasting fruit, so that the Father will give you whatever you ask for, using my name. This is my command: Love each other. (John 15:9–17, NLT)

One of my favorite quotes from the Hispanic pastor, Yesenia Then, from her book, *Mujer Reposiciónate: Revela tu diseño y no Dejes que Nada te Robe la Esencia*, is

> «Te conviertes en autoridad de aquello que vences, pero lo que te vence a ti, se convierte en autoridad tuya». Por tanto, el pleito verdaderamente termina cuando la batalla, la ganas tú. Y precisamente, para que la ganes tú, el Señor ha puesto sobre ti la unción que pudre yugos, rompe cadenas y destruye la iniquidad desde la misma cabeza. «Con tu fuerza puedo aplastar a un ejército; con mi Dios puedo escalar cualquier muro». Salmos 18:29 (NTV). (Yesenia Then)
>
> You become the authority of what you decide to (beat, conquer, overcome) but what (beats, conquers, overcomes) you, will become your authority. Therefore, the lawsuit really ends when you win the battle. And precisely, so that you win it, the Lord has put on you the anointing that rots yokes, breaks chains and destroys wickedness from the same head. "In your strength I can crush an army; with my God I can scale any wall (Psalms 18:29, NLT)." (Yesenia Then)

It's imperative that we understand that the enemy has a sneaky way of slithering into our minds to kill, steal, and destroy in the form of condemnation. He is an expert at reminding us of our past, of all the mistakes we've made, of all the people we've hurt, of all the things we could have or should have done. "With condemnation there's no transformation" (Pastor David Blunt).

Satan knows that if he can trap us into feeling guilty or ashamed, our focus will become distorted. This opens the door to confusion, doubt, discouragement—anything that renders us defenseless. As a result, we are hindered in such a way that we are unable to hear the voice of God. His goal is to bring a disconnection between you and God. He wants to kill our faith, our trust, and our belief in God. Ultimately, he wants you to walk condemned and defeated.

He's such a master at slithering false thoughts into our minds in order to influence us to question the heart of God.

When the deceiver Satan comes to slide himself into your soul to speak of things that condemn you and make you feel unworthy; quickly turn to the Word of God and speak it out loud.

> "No weapon that is formed against you will succeed; And every tongue that rises against you in judgment you will condemn. This [peace, righteousness, security, and triumph over opposition] is the heritage of the servants of the Lord, And this is their vindication from Me," says the Lord. (Isaiah 54:17, AMP)

From the book *Fervent: A Woman's Battle Plan to Serious, Specific, and Strategic Prayer*, it is stated this way:

> The first makes you focus on yourself; the other points you to the grace and empowering mercy of Christ. To hear the devil tell it, these weaknesses of yours are reason for nothing but wretched despair; yet God says those same weaknesses are reason for your purest worship and gratitude. Your need for God's grace is supposed to be a passion enhancer. That's the opposite of what takes place, however, as soon as you start believing the enemy's accusations. He'll make you think God doesn't hear your prayers or respond to them—why?—because of you. (Priscilla Shirer)
>
> My dear children, I am writing this to you so that you will not sin. But if anyone does sin,

we have an advocate who pleads our case before the Father. He is Jesus Christ, the one who is truly righteous. (1 John 2:1, NLT)

Let His Word cover your mind until there is no room for Satan's thorns. Engrave into your soul that you are loved and chosen. You have been delivered and set free. You have been forgiven and set apart for a purpose. Your past no longer defines you nor does it have power over you; Jesus has paid the full prize for your redemption. You are no longer condemned.

For God so [greatly] loved and dearly prized the world, that He [even] gave His [One and] only begotten Son, so that whoever believes and trusts in Him [as Savior] shall not perish, but have eternal life. For God did not send the Son into the world to judge and condemn the world [that is, to initiate the final judgment of the world], but that the world might be saved through Him. Whoever believes and has decided to trust in Him [as personal Savior and Lord] is not judged [for this one, there is no judgment, no rejection, no condemnation]. (John 3:16-18 AMP)

God is your loving Father, and Jesus is your elder brother who intercedes for you and me. The Holy Spirit is our helper in everything, and we are worthy of being a part of a family that nothing on earth or in heaven can separate.

We are going to experience many painful and difficult things here in this world. There will be times when the Word of God may not give you a clear-cut answer to the questions you seek or to the problem you face. But in those times, you can hold onto His promises. They will help guide you during those times of uncertainties.

And like what my pastor, David Blunt, says, "When you can't see God's hand, trust His heart."

> For everyone has sinned; we all fall short of God's glorious standard. Yet God, in his grace, freely makes us right in his sight. He did this through Christ Jesus when he freed us from the penalty for our sins. (Romans 3:23–24, NLT)

$\mathcal{J}$OY IGNITED IN DELIGHT

Have compassion on me, Lord, for I am weak. Heal me, Lord, for my bones are in agony. I am sick at heart. How long, O Lord, until you restore me? Return, O Lord, and rescue me. Save me because of your unfailing love. I am worn out from sobbing. All night I flood my bed with weeping, drenching it with my tears. My vision is blurred by grief; my eyes are worn out because of all my enemies. (Psalm 6:2–7, NLT)

Delight yourself also in the Lord, and He will give you the desires and secret petitions of your heart. (Psalm 37:4, AMPC)

GOD, HOW DO I take great pleasure in You and fully enjoy being in Your presence in the midst of this awful pain? How do I walk through this unimaginable rugged road of obstacles and still find happiness in You?

These were the questions I used to ask of the Lord after being tired of hiding my pain from people, and feeling like I had to put on a happy face so that I would not burden others with my troubles. I wanted to go through this journey in a manner where people could see firsthand through my story what it meant to experience heartbreak, yet still be able to rejoice in the Lord. And this is what I dis-covered; First, we must discipline our minds in such a manner that the Holy Spirit has total control.

> Now the mind of the flesh [which is sense and reason without the Holy Spirit] is death [death that comprises all the miseries arising from sin, both here and hereafter]. But the mind of the [Holy] Spirit is life and [soul] peace [both now and forever]. [That is] because the mind of the flesh [with its carnal thoughts and purposes] is hostile to God, for it does not submit itself to God's Law; indeed it cannot. So then those who are living the life of the flesh [catering to the appetites and impulses of their carnal nature] cannot please or satisfy God, or be acceptable to Him. But you are not living the life of the flesh, you are living the life of the Spirit, if the [Holy] Spirit of God [really] dwells within you [directs and controls you]. But if anyone does not possess the [Holy] Spirit of Christ, he is none of His [he does not belong to Christ, is not truly a child of God (Rom. 8:14).] (Romans 8:6–9, AMPC)
>
> So then, brethren, we are debtors, but not to the flesh [we are not obligated to our carnal nature], to live [a life ruled by the standards set up by the dictates] of the flesh. For if you live according to [the dictates of] the flesh, you will surely die. But if through the power of the [Holy] Spirit you are [habitually] putting to death (mak-ing extinct, deadening) the [evil] deeds prompted by the body, you shall [really and genuinely] live forever. (Romans 8:12–13, AMPC)

The flesh will automatically be driven to satisfy the needs of its nature which is connected to sin. When our minds are preoccupied with our painful state, our flesh consequently looks for relief, for something to replace the ache. However, the alternatives offered are never lasting nor fulfilling; they actually bring more "misery." It's what I call the *placebo joy*. It's never the real thing, and that's why, after a while, we feel empty again. On the other hand, when we "habitually" conquer our fleshly desires through the power of the Holy Spirit and "make extinct" those thoughts that are toxic to our mental health, we are able to experience true joy and peace, no matter the valley we are in.

When we discipline our minds to stay on thoughts that bring peace, thoughts that trust in God's faithfulness, and in His matchless love, our spirit rejoices. Why? Because that state of mind is being controlled by the Holy Spirit. When the Spirit is in control, He releases life-giving sustenance that will automatically lead you to experience the fulfilling fruit of joy.

Once your mind is grounded in this truth, you will be able to put into practice some life-giving principles.

> O Lord, how long will you forget me? Forever? How long will you look the other way? How long must I struggle with anguish in my soul, with sorrow in my heart every day? How long will my enemy have the upper hand? But I trust in your unfailing love. I will rejoice because you have rescued me. I will sing to the Lord because he is good to me. (Psalm 13:1–6, NLT)

First, trust and believe without a doubt that Jesus loves you beyond measure. He proved it with His very own life.

If you trust that He loves you like no other, you are able to push past your pain and go to church, worship, serve, and fellowship with your church family with a joyful attitude (Psalm 5:7–8, NLT).

Believe that you are not alone. God sees and feels your pain and cares deeply about your well-being (Psalm 31:7 NLT).

If you trust in Him, you can rejoice because your convictions will be a reminder that no matter what you are facing today, God is always good. He will never do anything to harm you, rather He will stand up, be your recompense, and bring you out of despair into a new season of laughter (Psalm 5:11, AMPC).

If you trust that He is your counselor, protecting you as He clears a path for you, joy is inevitable (Psalm 32:8–11, NLT).

Second, you can delight in the Lord while in sorrow through a *heart of thanksgiving.*

> Thank [God] in everything [no matter what the circumstances may be, be thankful and give thanks], for this is the will of God for you [who are] in Christ Jesus [the Revealer and Mediator of that will]. (1 Thessalonians 5:18, AMPC)

In her book, *Daring Greatly*, Brené Brown, PhD, LMSW, talked about a research that she conducted where "gratitude emerged from the data as the antidote to foreboding joy. Participants described happiness as an emotion that's connected to circumstances, and they describe joy as a spiritual way of engaging with the world that's connected to practicing gratitude."

She further states that "practicing gratitude is how we acknowledge that there's enough and that we're enough."

This is confirmed in the Word of God:

> Why is everyone hungry for more? "More, more," they say. "More, more." I have God's more-than-enough, more joy in one ordinary day than they get in all their shopping sprees. At day's end I'm ready for sound sleep, For you, God, have put my life back together. (Psalm 4:6–7, MSG)

To be able to delight in the Lord, you have to undoubtedly believe that no matter what you are going through, no matter how much you have lost, God is more than enough. And if you have Him at the center of your life, you have all that you need.

Instead of placing our focus on what's wrong, on the unfortunate events that plague all of our lives at one moment or another, we can shift our perspective to view the good in what we still have left. So often, we take for granted the beauty, the treasures, the gifts, the opportunities we have until, sadly, they are no longer there. I have found that if we purposely take time to remove ourselves from unnecessary distractions, even if it's for a brief period of time, all of our senses become heightened. We surprisingly become aware of all the remarkable things that have been hidden by all of life's noises and disappointments.

So, my friend, I encourage you today to do some simple exercises that helped me be more grateful in any current state.

At the start of your day, say out loud the things that you're thankful for. Then continue throughout your day giving thanks for things like loved ones who are still in your life, having food to eat, having a roof over your head, for good health, for your job, etc., no matter how minuscule you think they may be. VOICE your gratitude. Another thing you can do is keep a gratitude journal next to your nightstand and before going to sleep, jot down a few of those things that brought a smile to your face during the day. Or keep a gratitude jar that you can fill with thankful notes you can share at dinner time with your family.

Doing practical exercises like these will send signals to your brain to release endorphins into your body which will result in happy emotions. (To learn more about this process, get Dr. Catherine Leaf's book, *Switch On Your Brain: The Key to Peak Happiness, Thinking, and Health*)

Third, speak life.

> I will praise You, O Lord, with my whole heart; I will show forth (recount and tell aloud) all Your marvelous works and wonderful deeds! I will rejoice in You and be in high spirits; I will sing praise to Your name, O Most High! When my enemies turned back, they stumbled and perished before You. The Lord also will be a refuge

and a high tower for the oppressed, a refuge and a stronghold in times of trouble (high cost, destitution, and desperation). And they who know Your name [who have experience and acquaintance with Your mercy] will lean on and confidently put their trust in You, for You, Lord, have not forsaken those who seek (inquire of and for) You [on the authority of God's Word and the right of their necessity]. [Ps. 42:1.] That I may show forth (recount and tell aloud) all Your praises! In the gates of the Daughter of Zion I will rejoice in Your salvation and Your saving help. (Psalm 9:1–3, 9–4, AMPC)

The Word of God says in Proverbs 18:21 that death and life is in the power of the tongue so, my friend, to experience the joy of the Lord, we must not speak death over our circumstances. We must avoid complaining and being critical over our trials, because in doing so, we are creating a spiritual barrier that prevents us from receiving God's blessings. Is this easy to do? *No.* I certainly had a difficult time finding ways to speak positive in the middle of my unexpected heartbreaking marriage crisis. However, I discovered that when I spoke life into my life and everything that I was facing, I became a *healthier* person in all aspects.

We don't have to wait until everything is as we want it to say, "Thank you, Jesus, for your goodness," "Thank you for your unfailing love," "Thank you for your loving kindness," "Thank you for your sustenance," "Thank you for being my daily bread and the reason that I live."

Why? Because if we truly love the Lord, then we can rejoice in Him, in *who* He is, what He means to us, and all that He has done for us, no matter the season we are in. You know you truly love Jesus when your heart is screaming with sharp pains, *yet* you open your mouth and give God praise.

Fourth, He delights in you.

> The Lord directs the steps of the godly. He delights in every detail of their lives. (Psalm 37:23, NLT)

It's an inexplicable feeling to know that the Author of Life and Death is captivated by every facet of our lives. Because of this very truth, we can be assured and rejoice that He will take great care and be active in what concerns us.

> You have turned my mourning into joyful dancing. You have taken away my clothes of mourning and clothed me with joy, that I might sing praises to you and not be silent. O Lord my God, I will give you thanks forever! (Psalm 30:11–12, NLT)

To experience springs of joy at the core of your being, establish a foundation where the source of joy is not motivated by people or circumstances, but the natural overflow of your delight in the Lord. YES, all in the EYE OF THE STORM.

God's gift of joy is so out of this world that you will find yourself free to *just be. Not perfect, not religious, but in a loving relationship with Jesus, and in an earthly journey of growth and transformation.* This is all part of God's unfailing love and blessings for His children.

> Jesus is the source of our joy, and He's the sustainer of it. Apart from Him, our lives are made up of empty, meaningless attempts to find satisfaction. We wander, desperately thirsty until we drink from Him. He's the beginning and the end, the Alpha and the Omega. Every good gift is from His hand, and nothing good exists apart from Him. Our desire for joy is ultimately a desire for Jesus. (Melissa B. Kruger, *In All Things*)

IT'S NOT OVER, GOD HAS A PREDESTINED PLAN

I FOUND MYSELF with a deep urgency to uncover what awaited me and my girls in the future. What our new life was going to look like from God's point of view. The uncertainties had my head spinning for answers because what was unfolding in my life seemed to contradict the human understanding of my faith.

My mind was in a whirlwind trying to make sense out of God's promises in the valley I was passing through, and the new path that laid before me. So I began a dialogue with the Holy Spirit, asking Him to reveal God's truth as it pertained to our future. My pastor, David Blunt, always reminded us not to look at our circumstances through the experiences of other people. Thus, I sought specific answers about what God's plan was for my family.

The Bible says,

> Many plans are in a man's mind, but it is the Lord's purpose for him that will stand. [Job 23:13; Psalm 33:10–11; Isaiah 14:26–27, 46:10; Acts 5:39; Hebrews 6:17] (Proverbs 19:21, AMPC)
>
> But once he has made his decision, who can change his mind? Whatever he wants to do, he does. So he will do to me whatever he has

planned. He controls my destiny. (Job 23:13–14, NLT)

The Lord destroys the plans and spoils the schemes of the nations. But what the Lord has planned will stand forever. His thoughts never change. (Psalm 33:10–11, CEV)

I have planned this for the whole world, and my mighty arm controls every nation. I, the Lord All-Powerful, have made these plans. No one can stop me now! (Isaiah 14:26–27, CEV)

Only I can tell you the future before it even happens. Everything I plan will come to pass, for I do whatever I wish. (Isaiah 46:10, NLT)

Now in the present case let me say to you, stand off (withdraw) from these men and let them alone. For if this doctrine or purpose or undertaking or movement is of human origin, it will fail (be overthrown and come to nothing); But if it is of God, you will not be able to stop or overthrow or destroy them; you might even be found fighting against God! (Acts 5:38–39, AMPC)

God also bound himself with an oath, so that those who received the promise could be perfectly sure that he would never change his mind. So God has given both his promise and his oath. These two things are unchangeable because it is impossible for God to lie. Therefore, we who have fled to him for refuge can have great confidence as we hold to the hope that lies before us. This hope is a strong and trustworthy anchor for our souls. It leads us through the curtain into God's inner sanctuary. Jesus has already gone in there for us. He has become our eternal High Priest in the order of Melchizedek. (Hebrews 6:17–20, NLT)

In my fervent search for answers, these scriptures confirmed various truths we can all place out complete faith in:

One, no matter what happens to us, God's ultimate plan will come to pass.

Two, God never changes His mind.

Three, God cannot lie.

Fourth, God is bound by His Word; therefore always keeps His promises.

Fifth, only God knows the end from the beginning.

Six, God is always in control over the earth and over our lives regardless of the circumstances.

Seven, God has a predestined plan for each and one of us.

What this means specifically for you and me is that when He says in His Word:

> "For I know the plans I have for you," says the Lord. "They are plans for good and not for disaster, to give you a future and a hope. (Jeremiah 29:11, NLT)
>
> For we are God's masterpiece. He has created us anew in Christ Jesus, so we can do the good things he planned for us long ago. (Ephesians 2:10, NLT)

It means that we were not born by sheer coincidence. God brought you and I to this earth with a foreseen plan in mind. Not just any plan but a plan where we have hope, goodness, and a future.

Nevertheless, the question many of us are asking is, if God's plan for me is for good, then why in the world am I going through so much heartache?

> God makes everything happen at the right time. Yet none of us can ever fully understand all he has done, and he puts questions in our minds about the past and the future. (Ecclesiastes 3:11, CEV)

Personally, here is where I stand with that question; Personally, I have come to terms that it does no good looking for something or someone to blame or try to figure out things that are out of a humans' ability to grasp. What we can do, nonetheless, is take responsibility for the decisions we've made, and ownership for the part we played in the way our lives turned out. Then...we turn it all over to God to reorder our steps and bring order into our chaos. This shift in perspective can help us begin to see our current situation and our destiny from God's perspective.

God's Word confirms that He already foresaw what we are currently facing; it's not news to Him. He was fully aware that you and I would walk through dark valleys, and purposely made provisions that would enable us to get through them, be internally transformed, and come out triumphant. If we stay in faith, if we stay in obedience, and if we trust Him, God will allow us to see miracles happen before our very own eyes.

Things in our lives may not have happened the way we planned, but we don't need to live in regret, guilt, or shame. Why? Because the Bible says, "For God's gifts and his call can never be withdrawn" (Romans 11:29, NLT).

This means, you still have a purpose and no matter what has happened, nothing can change that. God already set out a specific plan for you and I, and it's our responsibility to seek it, find it, and live it out to our fullest capacity in Christ Jesus.

I can look back and deem my life from the viewpoint of regret, or I can choose to look back and see my life through the sacrifice of Jesus. I can choose to see my past as a waste of time, or I can choose to see it as a period of transformation to the remarkable that lies ahead.

> I will tell them, "God's love can always be trusted,
> and his faithfulness lasts as long as the heavens."
> (Psalm 89:2, CEV)
> Trust in the Lord always, for the Lord God
> is the eternal Rock. (Isaiah 26:4, NLT)

We must remember that our circumstances do not define us, nor do they separate us from God's love nor can they steal our predestined purpose. No matter what we go through, we must always trust God. He promised to be there for us and "withhold nothing good from those who trust Him."

So whatever you do, keep moving forward and don't wallow in things that can't be undone. God promised to give you a good future. Believe it.

> Satisfy us each morning with your unfailing love, so we may sing for joy to the end of our lives. Give us gladness in proportion to our former misery! Replace the evil years with good. Let us, your servants, see you work again; let our children see your glory. And may the Lord our God show us his approval and make our efforts successful. Yes, make our efforts successful! (Psalm 90:14–17, NLT)
>
> But He said, Blessed (happy and to be envied) rather are those who hear the Word of God and obey and practice it! (Luke 11:28, AMPC)
>
> Now to Him Who, by (in consequence of) the [action of His] power that is at work within us, is able to [carry out His purpose and] do superabundantly, far over and above all that we [dare] ask or think [infinitely beyond our highest prayers, desires, thoughts, hopes, or dreams]– (Ephesians 3:20, AMPC)

A FAIRY TALE WITH A DIFFERENT ENDING

As evening came, Jesus said to his disciples, "Let's cross to the other side of the lake." So they took Jesus in the boat and started out, leaving the crowds behind (although other boats followed). But soon a fierce storm came up. High waves were breaking into the boat, and it began to fill with water. Jesus was sleeping at the back of the boat with his head on a cushion. The disciples woke him up, shouting, "Teacher, don't you care that we're going to drown?" When Jesus woke up, he rebuked the wind and said to the waves, "Silence! Be still!" Suddenly the wind stopped, and there was a great calm. Then he asked them, "Why are you afraid? Do you still have no faith?" (Mark 4:35–40, NLT)

I HAVE READ this passage many times before but it was not until my own personal storm and the revelation of the Holy Spirit that I understood what Jesus wanted the disciples to take to heart. As I read the passage, I could clearly picture myself on that boat along with the disciples, moving frantically, scared to bare bones about what might be our fate. All of my fears flooded my mind with force. *What will become of me? Of us? Of them?*

Yes, just like the disciples, when I first entered into my own *storm*, I said those similar words, "Teacher, don't you care that we're going to drown?"

Yes, He very much cares. But not every story has the same ending. And that is okay because that's how God orchestrates. The hardest part is accepting that our story will have an unexpected finale. The great news is that our story is not over; it has a continuation to look forward to.

Today, I have a different picture in my mind when I read this passage. I am still in the middle of a ferocious storm. I don't know what's going to be the end result, but instead of being anxious, worried, and full of fear, I am choosing to lie right next to Jesus. For this time, I put my trust in the One who, with one word, can calm any raging sea.

> To everything there is a season, and a time for every matter or purpose under heaven. (Ecclesiastes 3:1, AMPC)
>
> A time to weep and a time to laugh, a time to mourn and a time to dance. (Ecclesiastes 3:4, AMPC)

My friends, it's very important for us to remember that we can be the most perfect person on this earth, the most holy, righteous, giving, helpful, and the wisest, but no matter how good we think we are or try to be, you and I will still face seasons of drought. Nevertheless, there's great news. If we are in Christ Jesus, we can be confident that we will also experience seasons of abundance, calm, and harvest.

There will be unavoidable times in your life where you will experience mourning and much crying, but keep at the forefront of your mind, it is only temporary—it's only a season. In due time, there will be laughter and dancing to be held and enjoyed.

> For you have been born again, but not to a life
> that will quickly end. Your new life will last for-
> ever because it comes from the eternal, living
> word of God. (1 Peter 1:23, NLT)

My dear friends, I want to close this book with these final words; About two years ago, I entered into the toughest season of my life. It was so profound, at one point, I thought my life was over. I truly didn't know how I would overcome. But I am here to tell you that I did. How? With the love of my Heavenly Father, with the Grace of Jesus, the help of the Holy Spirit, and the support and encouragement of my dear mother and close friends. When I had received Jesus as my personal Savior years ago, I instantly became born again; however, after conquering this life-altering storm, I have experienced being born again internally. This time, through the power of the Holy Spirit, I have been filled with an inexplicable peace and joy. I have fully placed my hope in the fact that my "new life will last forever." I am no longer afraid of what lies ahead.

I am a testament that God can take broken pieces that have been tossed and trashed and make them into a beautiful art form He can use for His glory.

The events in your life may not change in the way you had so desperately prayed, fasted, and perhaps, went to immeasurable length to bring it to pass. Don't be downcast. Don't blame God or anyone else, including yourself. Don't focus on what you can't change; rather, trust that God has the perfect plan to see you through it and give you a new script to your story.

If you find yourself in the worst season of your life, don't panic; help is on the way. Follow the principles I shared with you and watch the Lord go to work in your life and in your circumstance. One way or another, things will turn around. You will smile again.

I pray the Holy Spirit fills your entire being with such joy, happiness and laughter that their overflow spills into every area of your life regardless of the circumstances you may face. May the Lord help you walk in this world in such a way that when you look back at the past, you simply smile, not at the perfection of your steps, but rather, at the beauty of what He has done with your imperfect ones.

And yes, you can and will overcome.

> You may have invested your life in your family, and from the looks of it, all is for naught. But perhaps the beauty of what your efforts have produced will not truly be seen until a later time. God has promised to repay us for the years the locusts have eaten. Don't be discouraged. Trust God. The future may hold treasures that are completely hidden from you now, but in God's perfect timing they will one day be revealed. He will yet fill your mouth with laughter and your lips with shouts of joy. —Job 8:21 (Linda Rooks)
>
> I waited patiently for the Lord to help me, and he turned to me and heard my cry. He lifted me out of the pit of despair, out of the mud and the mire. He set my feet on solid ground and steadied me as I walked along. He has given me a new song to sing, a hymn of praise to our God. Many will see what he has done and be amazed. They will put their trust in the Lord. I take joy in doing your will, my God, for your instructions are written on my heart. (Psalm 40:1– NLT)

ABOUT THE AUTHOR

DENISE RIAÑO HAS a Bachelor's degree in Social Work and a Minors in Religion from Southeastern University. She also has a Master's degree in Mental Health from Webster University. Denise is the Founder of 3Core Inner Wellness, a faith based platform used to help and empower people experience wellness in their body, soul and spirit.

Denise is the mother of two amazing and beautiful daughters, and is a woman whose passion is to serve God and use her gifts to make a difference in others. Her desire is to use her story and her service to be a voice of encouragement, hope and healing to the brokenhearted. She is on a mission to inspire others to grow, overcome, and to fulfill their own predestined destiny.

CPSIA information can be obtained
at www.ICGtesting.com
Printed in the USA
LVHW092240111219
640224LV00001B/96/P

9 781644 923542